LIVES
 ENTRUSTED

OTHER TITLES IN

PRISMS

Beyond the Scandals
G. Lloyd Rediger

The Church Enslaved
Michael Battle and Tony Campolo

Clergy Burnout
Fred Lehr

Healing Bodies and Souls
W. Daniel Hale and Harold G. Koenig

Lives Entrusted
Barbara J. Blodgett

Moving beyond Church Growth
Mark Olson

Open-Hearted Ministry
Michael Koppel

A Servant's Manual
Michael W. Foss

Spiritual Maturity
Frank A. Thomas

Transforming Leadership
Norma Cook Everist and Craig L. Nessan

Turn Your Church Inside Out
Walter Kallestad

LIVES

 ENTRUSTED

An Ethic of Trust for Ministry

Barbara J. Blodgett

Fortress Press
MINNEAPOLIS

LIVES ENTRUSTED
An Ethic of Trust for Ministry

Cover image: photo © 1998 MaryBeth Thielhelm/Photodisc/Getty Images
Cover design: Christy J. P. Barker
Book design: James Korsmo

Library of Congress Cataloging-in-Publication Data

Blodgett, Barbara J., 1961–
  Lives entrusted : an ethic of trust for ministry / Barbara J. Blodgett.
    p. cm. — (Prism series)
  Includes bibliographical references and index.
  ISBN 978-0-8006-6321-6 (alk. paper)
  1. Trust—Religious aspects—Christianity. 2. Interpersonal relations—Religious aspects—Christianity. I. Title.
  BV4597.53.T78B56 2008
  253—dc22
                                                            2008022278

The paper used in this publication meets the minimum requirements of American National Standard for Information Sciences—Permanence of Paper for Printed Library Materials, ANSI Z329.48-1984.

Manufactured in the U.S.A.

12   11   10   09   08   1   2   3   4   5   6   7   8   9   10

Contents

✺ INTRODUCTION

This book is about communities of faith and their leaders, and it argues that they should better learn how to practice trust. I will argue that healthy and prudent trust relationships are indispensable to communities of faith and that many of the moral problems that plague communities of faith are related to failures of trust. Trust is indispensable for this reason: to be a Christian is to live as part of a body, and the parts need always to be developing their relationships with one another. One main reason communities of faith are plagued by failures of trust, I argue, is because we take trust for granted and do not work at trust relationships. We too often settle for overly easy modes of relating, like gossip and spin, that prevent or undermine trust. Or we put our trust in policies and procedures rather than in people. This book will draw attention to the trust we take for granted and show how we can learn to practice it in smarter ways.

Some books on ministerial ethics focus solely on the ethical behavior or character of ministers and do not address the ethics of faith communities. It is not new to argue that ministerial leaders must be trustworthy. Recent revelations of ministerial sexual abuse may have heightened our awareness of the virtue of trustworthiness, but we have always claimed it as an important character trait in our leaders. This book instead focuses on the demands of living in relationship—including the relationships community members have with one other. To that end, trust is understood here as a relationship rather than a quality of individuals.

Trust is commonly understood as a noun, referring either to the environment or atmosphere in which we act or to the emotion or feeling that inspires how we act. In contrast, I examine trust as a verb. It is something

1

people *do*; it is an action, however consciously or unconsciously undertaken. More precisely, trust is a *trans*action that establishes a relationship. People entrust each other with things they value, and this bonds them together in caring for the valued thing. As a transaction, trust is something people can practice.

I first became interested in trust as a result of prior interest in the morality of actions like lying, whistle blowing, and secrecy. At first, my aim was to wrestle with traditional questions of right and wrong, for example, whether it was ever right to lie to another person. Then, I sought to figure out whether the ethics varied according to the context of the relationship, for example, whether a certain lie would be morally permissible in a personal relationship but not in a professional one or vice versa. This led to my seeing the indispensable connection between the morality of our actions and the quality and character of the relationships we wish to sustain. Actions, I realized, had to be judged in large part on the basis of whether they increased or decreased interpersonal trust. Increasingly, I became fascinated by instances whereby actions that might otherwise be deemed wrong nevertheless did *not* cause trust to diminish between people, as when, for example, one friend lied to another but the lie ironically strengthened their friendship. (I often tell the story that, at the time I became interested in trust as a scholarly topic, I had a mechanic who on more than one occasion told me he did not know what was wrong with my car. His failure to fix my car, combined with his transparency about it, actually made him a better mechanic in my eyes.) It was from this sort of irony that I decided trust must be an action in and of itself with its own ethics. That was how I embarked on the project of writing about the ethics of trust.

As I became trained to notice the often counterintuitive nature of trust, I also became increasingly interested in those actions that initially appear morally harmless—gossip and bullshit—as well as those actions that people tend not to question—keeping confidences and implementing safe church measures. Eventually these four different topics merged in my mind under the rubric of trust.

The book is arranged into five chapters. Chapter 1 defines trust and explains how it works between individuals and within communities. I argue that trust always involves risk, vulnerability, and power. We can therefore develop an ethic for trust relationships based on the principles that any risk should be appropriate to the trust relationship, any vulnerability be acknowledged and accepted by both truster and entrusted, and that the power between them be balanced as much as possible.

Chapter 2 takes up the issue of confidentiality in the ministry. I challenge the popular perception that ministers should keep silent everything they hear. I argue that this perception stems in large part from a "therapeutic model" of ministry that does not take the presence of community into account. Viewing confidentiality through the lenses of risk, vulnerability, and power, I point out the ways that confidants as well as confiders face certain risks. Ultimately I argue that while confidences should be carefully guarded once promised, ministers might start to promise confidentiality in fewer instances. This chapter thus invites us to imagine a community wherein ministers are not solely and unduly burdened with everyone else's secrets but, rather, where they facilitate relationships of appropriate vulnerability among those they serve.

Chapter 3 draws upon the work of Michael Power on the proliferation of "audit societies." Defining an audit as any means of checking up on a leader's work, and an audit society as any community that over-relies on audits to assure itself of the trustworthiness of its leaders, this chapter questions whether the church is in danger of becoming an audit society. It focuses on the increased use of verification procedures in the church for addressing the problem of ministerial misconduct and argues instead for practices that prevent misconduct by encouraging prudent trust.

Chapter 4 addresses gossip. Defined as informal conversation about others enjoyed at their expense, this chapter argues that gossip is not a form of pastoral care but, rather, an indirect and ultimately cowardly form of expression. It uses research from social psychology and gender studies to cast gossip as a strategy sought by those with less power to gain or resist it. People in faith communities would be better to learn the practice of testimony, which is direct and self-authored.

Chapter 5 deals with the temptation of clergy to bullshit. Defined in contrast to liars, bullshitters do not care one way or the other about the truth and deceive their listeners by pretending to be sincere and authentic. If gossip is female, bullshit is male. Bullshit, like gossip, is about power, but is used by those with power to retain it. Ecclesial bullshit takes the form of making easy what is not—talking meaningfully about Christian faith.

I have been fortunate in writing about topics that draw natural interest and curiosity from others. Over the years this project has developed, I have enjoyed many stimulating conversations with colleagues, students, and friends. In particular, I am indebted to students at Yale Divinity School and the Lay Ministers' School of the Christian Church (Disciples of Christ) in Kentucky. I also give thanks for my church, the Church of the Redeemer in New Haven, and for the broad-based organization of churches in New Haven formerly known as ECCO. It is a blessing to belong to good communities while writing about community.

Chapter One

✺ THE PRACTICE
OF TRUST

In Brian Moore's 1987 novel, *The Colour of Blood*, a priest becomes trapped in a world devoid of trust. The novel is a masterpiece not only of suspense but also of the themes of trust and power. Set in a fictitious communist bloc country before the fall of the Soviet Union, it begins with an assassination attempt on Cardinal Bem, the country's Roman Catholic cardinal. As the reader knows, historically, the Catholic Church had precarious relationships with different communist governments, and in this story, Cardinal Bem had been successful over the years maintaining a concordat between church and state, owing in part to his longstanding relationship with the prime minister, a boyhood Jesuit schoolmate. In this country, Catholics were allowed to practice their religion and even won from the state occasional concessions regarding human rights and freedoms, but the state maintained ultimate control. This did not please everyone. Some in the left wing of the Catholic Church thought Cardinal Bem had sold them out to the state. They wanted the church to resist the state more actively, even if it meant violent conflict. Now an attempt has been made on the cardinal's life and the question becomes: Who is behind it?

After narrowly escaping the assassination attempt, Bem is subsequently kidnapped from his residence in the capital by forces that pose as state security police (SP). They drive him to a farm far out in the countryside and claim to be taking him into custody for his own protection. They tell him that a radical group within his church is trying to kill him. Furthermore, they say, the radicals are planning to instigate an uprising among Catholics the following week after an annual holy day of pilgrimage to a place called Rywald, commemorating martyrs from two centuries ago. Cardinal Bem, still believing his captors to be the SP, privately concedes that they might be correct, as he has harbored his own suspicions about a possible insurrection, if not assassination. Nevertheless, he is dismayed that his captors have had access to such information while he has not.

> "And they would kill me?"
> "Some of them, yes. The lunatic fringe, I suppose."
> In the small cluttered office, the silence that followed was broken by the bumbling of a large housefly against the windowpane. The morning sun, summer hot, spilled across the overflowing correspondence trays on the colonel's desk. There is authority in what he says: he bathes daily in a running tap of words inspired by fear and greed, in secret reports of unwary talk, in denunciations inspired by hatred, words spoken after torture. It is the state's business to know these things. The church has no comparable intelligence.[1]

Cardinal Bem's captors do not pretend to respect him. In fact, they accuse him of having been corrupted by careerism, a desire to remain head of the church even to the point of compromising his ideals. He responds to these accusations:

> "No wonder you Communists cannot understand our people," he said. "You see everything through your own distorting mirror."
> "Do we?" the Major asked. "What does Your Eminence mean by that?"
> "I mean that power is your preoccupation, not mine."[2]

Desperate to head off a popular uprising against the state, and the arrests and violence that would inevitably follow, Bem evades his appointed "chaplain" the next afternoon when they are out on a walk. He is picked up on the road by local police, who do not recognize him, and gets dropped off in the nearby town. Realizing that in order to accomplish his mission he must go undercover, as it were, he removes and discards his collar and purple shirtfront, and takes off his ring.

> He was now a hunted man, sought by forces of the State who had tried to imprison him. He stared down into the gull-haunted canyon. Into his mind like a half-forgotten incantation came the words: *Pro nomine Jesu contumelias pati.* To suffer in Jesus' name. That is now my fate and

I must give thanks for it. My task is to serve You. For that task I must be free.[3]

Weary and afraid, he stumbles into a local church. Some women are setting the altar for mass and in an extraordinary coincidence, Bem recognizes one of them as the driver of the car whose passenger had tried to assassinate him the other night. He realizes with sickening clarity as he rushes back outside that the forces of resistance have indeed grown within his own church without his having known. Now he has enemies on all sides. Every town square, every café, even every church, is a potentially dangerous space and he does not know whom he can trust. Thus begins a nightmarish spiral of further arrests, escapes, subterfuge, and even a night spent sleeping among bums under a bridge. He calls an old friend who promises to send someone with money. A young man shows up, and Bem agrees to have coffee with him. Despite the fact that the man bears a note in his friend's handwriting, Bem cannot help but remain on his guard. "He had accepted this young man's story, yet it could be a trap. Suddenly, he did not feel like talking any more. This, he thought, is what life must be like for those who no longer trust each other."[4]

Bem manages to meet with the head of one of the nation's largest unions, where he learns that its leaders have not come out in support of the demonstration. The news is simultaneously hopeful and disturbing. Without union backing the demonstration is likely to fail, yet their lack of involvement confirms that another group is behind the plot. When he falls soon thereafter into police hands, Bem persuades them to take him to meet the prime minister. There he learns that a military barracks was bombed the day before and that a group called the Christian Fighters has claimed responsibility. The prime minister believes it is this group who kidnapped Bem. The two leaders talk, and establish a tentative accord: the police will let the cardinal go and promise not to hinder him for twenty-four hours, if in return he will make a public statement clearing the state of responsibility for his capture and try to avert a national uprising among his people.

Bem decides that the time for subterfuge is over and asks for a public escort back to his residence. He prays: "From now on, I must draw the danger toward me. As always, I am Your servant. Do with me what you will."[5] Once home, he tapes the promised statement for national television. After doing so, he lays a plan to confront the one bishop in his region, Bishop Krasnoy, whom he suspects of leading the resistance. Krasnoy's anti-West, anti-Rome convictions suggest that he might urge revolution against state power in the name of a free church. Finally returned to his familiar surroundings and reinstated in his role as the leader of the church, Bem nonetheless cannot shake the practice of wariness he developed while on the run. Even as his staff help him with the preparations, he realizes that he regards them differently. "He turned from Kris and looked at Finder. Was Finder to be trusted? Suddenly, he felt ashamed. Of course I must trust him. *As you would that men should do to you, do you also to them in like manner.*"[6]

The bishops have all been called in for an episcopal conference, and they arrive at the residence later that day. Bem seizes the opportunity to surprise them. Instructing his staff not to tell them he has returned, he steps into the room where they are gathered and quickly scans their faces for reaction. A glance between Krasnoy and another bishop confirms his worst fears. He soon learns that they have, indeed, been working to incite a national demonstration and had colluded in his detention by terrorists called the Christian Fighters.

All that remains is for Cardinal Bem to preside at the Rywald commemoration mass and deliver an impassioned plea to his people not to demonstrate against the state. However, the story does not end without one more twist of hidden identity and a final lethal threat. The reader waits, as if with Cardinal Bem himself, to learn the outcome.[7]

§ § §

The Colour of Blood invites us to imagine a world without trust. In this world, deception and secrecy are the norm, and honesty and openness actually abnormal. Trustworthy people are indistinguishable from the untrustworthy. Like the bleak and foul riverbank where the destitute hunker down under a bridge, the world into which Cardinal Bem plunges is filled with despair. The novel's frequent metaphors of darkness and abyss suggest that the loss of trust is like descending underground. Trust in others provides for human beings the very basis for our acting in the world—our sense of security, our relationships, and our ability to navigate through problems. Without it, life becomes despairing.

We begin our study of trust with a story about its absence because interpersonal trust is so often taken for granted. Indeed, our awareness of it is typically prompted only when we can no longer assume it. Moral philosopher and Hume scholar Annette Baier compares our assumption about trust to that of the air we breathe: "We inhabit a climate of trust as we inhabit an atmosphere and notice it as we notice air, only when it becomes scarce or polluted."[8] Cardinal Bem notices his own trust in others disappearing when he no longer has the impetus to talk to anyone. Having lost the capacity to discern whom to trust, he shuts down. Distrust of others freezes his confidence and his very ability to function.

When we *are* aware of the trust we have given others, we typically describe it as a feeling or emotion. We compare trust to love, intimacy, security, or comfort. In our references to it, trust is usually a noun. We think of it either as the background condition to our actions or the feeling accompanying them. Less frequently is trust contemplated as a verb. In this book I hope to persuade readers to regard trust as something we choose to *do* to be in relationship, not just something *about* a relationship that we experience. Moreover, I hope to persuade readers that trust is something we can get better at doing.

Indeed, another way to read Moore's novel is as the story of a man who progresses from naïveté to sophistication in trusting others. At the beginning, the novel shows him living the sheltered existence of a cardinal. His private life revolves around a residence where nearly all his basic needs are attended to by others, and in his everyday public life he exercises without hesitation the authority that comes with his title. In other words, he trusts people and is trusted by them with nearly unthinking ease. After the assassination attempt, we watch Bem gradually come to terms with his own lack of awareness. He realizes that he had been unduly shielded from hard realities within his church. He had remained ignorant of a plan for mutiny within the ranks of his own bishops. Toward the end of the story, we see a new Cardinal Bem emerge. When he returns to his residence he is not the same man who left. He has had to shed some of his former innocence, assume nothing from others' appearance, learn to distinguish enemy from friend, be sparing with information, and broker a deal with the prime minister in order to be entrusted with his own freedom. Once home, we see him inwardly assessing the trustworthiness of his staff, even as he regrets having to do so. He plays a mild trick on the bishops in order to test their loyalty. He plans his homily for Rywald with utmost care and confronts those who would prevent him from delivering it. In short, he takes trust less for granted and learns that it something he must employ with care.

In our attempt to reimagine trust as an activity we undertake, it would probably help if we used a distinct word. While "trust" can be a noun or a verb, "entrust" is always a verb. (I will, however, use the two terms interchangeably, meaning by "trust" the act of entrusting.) "To entrust" is, moreover, a transitive verb, a verb that requires a relationship and an action. When I entrust you with something, I transfer that something to you, and in so doing seal the two of us together in a relational bond. Trust is, if you will, a *trans*action. It is an action that changes relationship. Even when two people know each other very well, if one begins to entrust the other with new things, a new relationship is established between them. We will call this relationship a trust relationship.

To better understand trust is to understand the trust relationship. We now turn away, therefore, from a narrative description and toward a more direct philosophical examination of interpersonal trust. For those who might be apprehensive because they are unaccustomed to scrutinizing something as seemingly intuitive as trust, I would recall an important aspect of Cardinal Bem's journey. From a man who trusted others and received trust almost without question, Bem admittedly becomes someone who bestows it more selectively. He himself learns to scrutinize the simple act of trust. And yet his transformation from naïveté to discernment does not come about at the expense of his faith or his love for his people. This is crucial to note. In a different story, the captive might become a bitter man, as mean as his captors. Instead, Bem's growing sophistication in the ways of trust is fitted gracefully into his priestly character. He never loses his willingness to make sacrifices for Christ. He remains throughout a man of great kindness and remarkable humility. In biblical terms, he is still gentle as a dove even when he becomes wise as a serpent. If we would strive to increase not just the feeling of trust within our communities of faith, but also the sophistication and wisdom with which it is bestowed, we would do well to remember this. To practice smarter, better trust does not mean we will be forced to choose between kindness and shrewdness, faithfulness and pragmatism. Practicing genuine trust combines all of these.

THE PARADIGMATIC TRUST RELATIONSHIP

Let us begin our description of the trust relationship with an example familiar to philosophers as well as sociologists, game theorists, economists, and others who study the dynamics of human cooperation and trust. It is called the Prisoner's Dilemma. Imagine that there are two prisoners residing in separate prison cells who have been arrested for a jointly committed crime. The crime normally carries a sentence of five years upon conviction. In order to prosecute their case successfully and win a conviction, the authorities need one of the prisoners to betray the other, so the following deal is separately offered to both: if one of you betrays the other and the other does not betray you, you will walk free and the other will receive the five-year sentence. If you both choose to betray each other, you will not walk free but you will both receive only a three-year sentence. However, if neither of you betrays the other and both remain silent, you will still be sentenced but there will only be enough evidence to make you stay one year in prison.[9] Thus, the Prisoner's Dilemma can be schematized as follows:

	Prisoner B Stays Silent	Prisoner B Betrays
Prisoner A Stays Silent	Each serves 1 year	Prisoner A: 5 years Prisoner B: goes free
Prisoner A Betrays	Prisoner A: goes free Prisoner B: 5 years	Each serves 3 years

Table 1.1

Would most prisoners choose to remain silent or betray? The prosecutor's offer is designed to tempt the prisoners into betraying each other. Betrayal carries the enticing chance of freedom, but only at one's partner's expense. It may represent the "best" outcome for the individual but also represents hurting the other. Mutual silence makes possible a decent outcome for both, but only when chosen by both. It represents the best collective outcome. Is it reasonable to assume that one's partner will remain silent? Is trust a prudent choice?[10]

In workshops that I teach on trust, I use the Prisoner's Dilemma to help students experience trust as a chosen action. I ask them to play the game by pairing them off and giving each partner two cards, labeled Silence and Betrayal. On the count of three, refraining from any conversation, each partner lays down a card. Both learn in that moment whether they could count on the other for cooperation and be counted on by them—or not. Playing this game gives players a sense, however mild, of the experience of entrusting themselves to another. They grasp, most fundamentally, that trust is something they can decide to do. Beyond that, they discover that trust is an inevitably risky decision. When I ask players to describe the moment just before laying down their cards, they report a sense of tension, whether of excitement or apprehension or just plain curiosity. They say it felt like taking a risk, letting themselves be vulnerably open to the twin possibilities of emerging victorious or getting duped. Sometimes they remember feeling like they just had to hope for the best. They experienced, in other words, what it was like to have a choice (indeed, to *have* to make a choice) and yet not to be in control. I tell them they have just outlined the experience of trust. Finally, in recalling the moment of attempting to calculate what their partner will do, they describe trust as something that occurs within the context of a specific relationship. When playing the game, partners will usually pause and think about the relationship they have with each other. (I frequently notice them looking intently into each others' eyes, as if trying to send or receive a message, often smiling devilishly.) Sometimes they ponder how their relationship will change depending on the choice each makes.

A trust relationship is the kind of relationship created when one person hands over to another something of value (like their fate in court), for its safekeeping.[11] If we were to diagram it, the relationship would look like an arrow connecting three points: Person A entrusting Person B with Valued Thing C (A > C > B). This diagram, or formula, will therefore serve as our paradigm for trust. It does not perfectly reflect all trust relationships, but it captures most of the important features of trust. Let us consider a specific example. When I tell the members of my small group a guilty secret, I am doing more than sharing information with them. I am giving to them, for their wise handling, information about me that is sensitive to me. I become a truster. As Person A, I entrust them—in this case plural Persons B—with this "thing" of mine. (Frequently, as in this case, the Valued Thing C is not a literal thing but nevertheless something of value. My secret is certainly valuable to me though not strictly speaking a possession of mine.) Because it is valuable, and because I share it, my confession comes to symbolize the trust relationship among us.

The practice of entrusting thus means giving to someone else something of yours that you hold dear, for them to take care of for a while, or forever. Some mundane examples might include leaving your children with a babysitter, or giving your house key to a neighbor. But let us consider some more examples from the life of faith. A baby being baptized can be said to "give over" its spiritual health and welfare to the community. A seminarian entrusts her comprehension of the New Testament to her professor. A cardinal entrusts his bishops with the well-being of the church during a time of political unrest. A hospital patient entrusts her spiritual health to the chaplain who calls on her following an unexpected, undesirable diagnosis. Teenagers at First Congregational Church whose covenant includes "what happens in youth group stays in youth group" entrust each other with their doubts and vulnerabilities. In paradigmatic trust, Person A is an individual who deliberately decides to trust Person B. But as these examples show, Persons A and B might represent multiple people, for it is possible for groups to enter into trust relationships. In addition, the trust might be more or less deliberate.

The fate of Valued Thing C keeps the truster and entrusted bound together in relationship. Trust relationships are lived out over time; they have a beginning, middle, and sometimes, an end. The duration may be brief, as in seeking solace from a hospital chaplain you will never meet again, but the more interesting examples of trust last longer. As we shall see a bit later, the Prisoner's Dilemma game becomes even more interesting when players play it over and over again and thus compound their dilemma by recollecting their shared track record. In any event, the way Persons A and B continue to act toward one another, and toward C, further defines the nature of their relationship as one of trust. A trust relationship is necessarily characterized by an attitude of openness toward the future, and requires a measure of accepted ambiguity on the part of A with respect to how B will care for C.[12]

In the previous generation of scholars who studied trust, philosopher Niklas Luhmann's work stands out. Luhmann's fundamental premise was that trust in others provides humans with a way to reduce the inevitable complexity of their lives. He used the image of pruning: "The problem of trust therefore consists in the fact that the future contains far more possibilities than could ever be realized in the present. . . . Men must, therefore, prune the future so as to measure up with the present—i.e. reduce complexity."[13] We can never be sure what the future will bring, and so we learn to trust people as a way to navigate that uncertainty. We let go of our desire to investigate and forestall every possible eventuality, and trust that things will work out. Sometimes, people playing the Prisoners' Dilemma say that they chose to remain silent simply because it was the easiest option to remember! In some ways, trust does make things smoother.

Looking ahead for a moment to our discussion of truth telling, we might point out that life's complexity sometimes comes in the form of the mixed information we so often hear. We can appreciate the challenge of needing to "prune" myriad possibilities if we consider how hard it is sometimes to judge between competing sources of truth. We become bewildered and incapable of action. The challenge of discerning the truth is hard enough when the competition represents legitimate and credible points of view; when we become subject to spin and conjecture, matters are made even worse. As we shall see later in the chapter on "bullshit," people who bend and spin the truth harm us if only because they render it even harder for us to navigate uncertainty. They exacerbate the "pruning" task we already face in life.[14]

For now, it is important to note that entrusting others is but one way to prune the future of its unfolding possibilities and make things smoother. Other ways are more decisive, and we frequently choose them over trust. If one of the prisoners sent a spy into the other prisoner's cell to learn what choice he was making, the first prisoner would not be entrusting his fate to his partner but, rather, determining for sure how to act.[15] In our own lives, we attempt similar strategies, trying to ensure that certain favorable possibilities are more likely to succeed. We learn to make contracts and other kinds of formal agreements that help lock in future actions, as when we mount a pledge drive before setting the church's annual budget rather than entrusting the church's finances to people's generosity. (Even this involves some trust, as compared, say, to collecting everyone's actual contributions first.) At times we stipulate conditions such as deadlines, like when we place new volunteers on probation and do not necessarily agree to continue our relationship with them past a certain point. Finally, frequently we check back over actions we have previously taken to verify that their outcomes were as we expected—this is called auditing—as in making random checks on the nursery caregivers or annually reviewing the performance of our Sunday school teachers.

Ensuring possibilities, creating contracts, putting audits in place: while trust does not necessarily exclude such measures, they represent alternatives to the trust relationship, as I am defining it for the purposes of our discussion. When we choose to go the way of these strategies we likewise reduce complexity and contain the future. But the difference between them and trust is that trust deliberately embraces openness and the possibility of change. It accepts a measure of complexity by "go[ing] beyond the information it receives," as Luhmann puts it.[16] When we trust people, we put less stock in the factual evidence they can provide at any given time than on the wager we form with them regarding the future. We eschew the formality of investigations and contracts and do not bind them to act in the ways we stipulate. This is what it means to *trust* them.

And so, when I enter into a trust relationship, is it to become more secure, but I nevertheless give over some discretion to the person I trust.

I wager some, if not all, of my security. In this sense, therefore, trust is not the choice to take if making life smooth is the top priority. Trust can become a bumpy road to follow.

Knowing this, and depending on circumstances, sometimes people choose not to trust. They rightly hesitate before trusting the other. Like Cardinal Bem, who kept his identity secret except to the one individual whom he thought was trustworthy, they will not risk laying themselves open to consequences they cannot predict. This is fine, and often smart, for sometimes being able to see the evidence is too important. Choosing *not* to trust is not necessarily the lesser moral choice. In fact, choosing sometimes not to trust makes the trust we *do* bestow all the more meaningful.

We have already identified one central feature of the paradigmatic trust relationship: risk. Trusting others always involves *risk*. We go out on a limb, so to speak, when we trust someone else with something that matters to us. A second feature is *vulnerability*. Trusting other people always makes us in some way vulnerable to them. We open ourselves up to the possibility that harm will come to us or to the thing we value, however offset by the gains we hope to receive. A third feature is *power*. Trusting other people invites a shift in the balance of power between us and them. In some relationships this imbalance is never completely leveled, and the partners have to work to keep it balanced. These three features are central to an ethic of trust because morally good trust relationships keep all three in check: when a trust relationship is sound, risk is reasonable, vulnerability is accepted, and power differences are minimized. Therefore, these features will occupy us for most of the rest of the chapter. Let us examine them in turn.

RISK

That risk is an inevitable feature of trust we usually realize too late. Only when someone lets us down by taking advantage of our trust do we see the danger we had placed ourselves in all along. Hindsight, as they say, is 20/20: wisdom is clarified only when the moment we need it has passed. Philosophers, and others who study human phenomena like trust for a living, trade on that hard-won clarity. They tell us what at some level we have always known. In this case, they tell us that entering into a trust relationship involves risk because we wager our future.

Let us return to our example of my telling my small group a guilty secret. I take a risk, if for no other reason than the secret does not reflect well on me. When I take it, I probably do so because sharing the information relieves me of the burden or signals to my group that I need spiritual help. There is always a chance one of them will spill my secret, thus broadcasting my guilt to others outside our group whom I would rather did not know it. (Or perhaps worse, and just as likely in some churches, the inattentive group might ignore or minimize what I have said and fail to provide me any spiritual succor.) To entrust them with my secret is to accept the wager that I might feel even worse. If I trust them it means I decide that telling is worth it. In all likelihood, I have reason to suspect that my trust is prudent. There are some things I know: perhaps I have in the past shared many other things with these people that they have faithfully honored, or perhaps the mistake itself was not so scandalous so that the number of people outside our group who would care about it are few. But still there are things I do not—and cannot—know, such as the temptation one of them might face this particular time to disclose my secret in the name of a greater good, the help they might be able to offer me if they were to seek advice from someone outside, or the relief it might bring some third person to know that I was guilty of their same transgression. The point is that I act without being able to know just what will happen. When one has reached the limit of reliable information, one is forced to trust that things will turn out all right. Luhmann said: "Trust always extrapolates from the available knowledge; it is . . . a blending of knowledge and ignorance."[17]

If I could look into the proverbial crystal ball and know exactly what my group would do with my information, then it would not be trust I chose but something else, like a test. In other words, if I know the people I trust so well that I can confidently predict what they will do, then properly speaking, my trust is minimal. Note that this is a different understanding of trust than we may be used to. Typically we associate minimal risk with generous trust, as when a person says of her best friend, "I can trust her with anything." It might seem that our concern would always be to minimize risk. However, as we will see at various points in this book, sometimes people should be encouraged to take a little *more* risk. Here we are correlating risk and trust in the opposite way: the greater the risk, the greater the trust. We are saying that entering a trust relationship always includes some risk. If risk is one feature of trust, then trust will grow when people take a risk. Gossipers, for example, who dare to stop gossiping and try instead to speak their minds directly and forthrightly take a risk, but it is a good risk to take! Similarly, preachers take a risk when they forgo the temptation to spin entertaining stories in their sonorous "pulpit voices" and choose instead to share honest words from their hearts. While nobody can predict with full certainty the risks that might be encountered, prudent trusters and trustees take risk into account even as they go ahead and form trust relationships.

This is important when we consider the practice of confidentiality. Church members will grow in mutual trust only when they risk revealing themselves to each other. Think about it. A church where no one takes any risks is a church where relationships remain formal and distant. (At the same time, of course, a church that puts no boundaries around risk is a church where relationships quickly dissolve. A small group ministry will generally be strengthened, for example, by shared guidelines about what stays in the group and what does not.) Growing in trust will mean accepting a certain amount of unpredictability and not forcing people to pass a test.

The other trust relationships cited earlier likewise all involved risk. The church might fail to fulfill its baptismal promises, the seminary professor might decide to use the classroom to promote propaganda, the bishops might mutiny, the chaplain might compound the patient's grief by mouthing platitudes about God's will, and the teenagers might gossip about each other outside of youth group. In each case, somebody goes out on a limb with somebody else.

In the act of entrusting, there are two things trust is *not*: neither familiarity nor reliance. It is important to note that trust is not simply the same as familiarity. People perpetually confuse the two and think that entrusting someone automatically comes with knowing them well. The confusion is understandable, for familiarity certainly reduces the risk associated with trust. Prisoner's Dilemma players tend to do better when they know each other. Cardinal Bem's trust in the prime minister rested in part upon connections they had going all the way back to their youth in Catholic school together. Yet familiarity does not by itself spell trust. Not only do we sometimes trust total strangers, but we also sometimes pause before trusting even those closest to us. Even with those well known to us, trust is still like going out on a limb. Trust introduces a new dynamic even to relationships of long standing. If anything, trust results in greater familiarity rather than the other way around. Ultimately we run a risk even with those people we know intimately if we entrust them with something we care about. This is important for people in the church to remember, so that they do not take their familiarity with each other for granted ("She's been a member here for years. We can trust her.").

Neither is trust the same thing as reliance. It is more than counting on others to be obedient. When I trust you, I expect something other than your adherence to certain rules I have set down. Indeed, if I believed that you and I had a relationship characterized by trust, and subsequently discovered that you had just been following a set of instructions in your behavior toward me, I would be justified in my disappointment. Trustworthiness cannot be locked in by rules, or else it is not really trustworthiness but something else. This will become relevant to our discussion of safe church measures, taken to try to ensure the trustworthiness of clergy. Many of these measures amount basically to establishing specific, predictable rules and practices that are deemed safe. People in churches, as everywhere else, tend to believe that if they can anticipate regular patterns of behavior in their leaders, they have trust, and their leaders are trustworthy. We can appreciate this assumption, especially from communities with a history of discovering shockingly aberrant behavior among their leaders. The instinctive response thereafter *would* be to establish standard practices and check up to be sure everyone is following them. Under the influence of these stories, it can be difficult to remember that trustworthiness is not the same as consistency. Not only can a leader consistently follow the practices laid down while finding ways to misbehave around them, but on occasion trustworthiness means breaking a rule in the interest of doing the right thing. All the rules in the world cannot ensure trustworthiness, for while trust is an action, it is foremost a relationship.[18]

When we trust others, therefore, we do not merely trade on either the familiarity or the rules that pertain between us. Trust is a unique sort of relationship because of the risk it incorporates. Again, the example of telling my small group a guilty secret is instructive. When I tell them, I initiate a special link among us. They receive something from me that they know I care about, and I know they know this. The information is still mine, but now it is theirs as well. Within the normal practices associated with small group ministry, they can do what they will, such as sharing their own confessions to shed further light on my situation. (If for some reason they were to step outside normal practices, they could do even more, like attempting armchair psychoanalysis with me.) We share an understanding of all this without even mentioning it. Thoughts of what might happen with regard to my/our secret pass between us unspoken. The bond of trust is initiated without any attention drawn—which is what makes it trust—and yet it holds us together by virtue of the exchange that was risked.

Trust relationships are truly fascinating in this way, for they involve both an awareness of risk and a decision to ignore that awareness. Philosopher Annette Baier writes of trusting as requiring "awareness of one's confidence that the trusted will not harm one, although they could harm one" as well as a twofold renunciation: "renunciation of guard or defense and renunciation of intelligence."[19] She calls it renunciation rather than reduction because she believes that a truster cannot continue to remind the trusted of her confidence. A truster can only say, "I'm trusting you, remember!" so many times before it ceases to feel like trust. She has to set aside—that is, renounce—suspicions about others' untrustworthiness if she is fully to trust them. She even has to set aside thoughts about her confidence in their trustworthiness! Trust is truly *accepted* risk.

Consequently, if we want a trust relationship to last, we must check our temptation constantly to look after how things go. We cannot keep too close an eye on the people we trust, or trust will quickly die. Cardinal Bem knew this when he felt ashamed for suspecting his loyal assistant, Finder. If, despite all that had happened, he still wanted a trust relationship with Finder, he knew he must follow the Golden Rule and extend the benefit of the doubt. We must be willing to suspend our inclination to monitor or audit the people we want to trust. Indeed, we could say the essence of trust lies in our willingness to relinquish the chance to check up on and direct the other's behavior, at least initially if not forever.[20]

VULNERABILITY

If risk is one identifying feature of interpersonal trust, then an accompanying feature is vulnerability. Like risk, the fact that vulnerability is always associated with trusting we tend to discover too late, in the aftermath of a trust relationship gone bad. People who are not good at trusting often realize too late that they put themselves in a vulnerable situation. Their dismay finds voice in a common lament: "I thought I *knew* you." Here, the pain of betrayal is expressly connected to the familiarity they (thought they) had with the trusted. For as we have seen, the better we come to know another person, the more we tend to "trust" them. But greater trust actually means exposing ourselves to greater harm.

Therefore, now that we have accepted a definition of trust as accepted risk, we can be even more specific: trust is accepted risk of vulnerability to another's possible harm. *The Colour of Blood* illustrates very well the vulnerability a truster incurs. Cardinal Bem consciously accepts his own vulnerability when he takes off and discards his collar and purple shirt and hides his ring—the symbols of authority that give him power to act in the world as a cardinal and not just an ordinary citizen. Through these deliberately chosen actions, he accepts the danger in which he has been placed. Bem, however, is able to transform that danger into freedom by reframing it as service to God. Stripped of the symbols of his power, he becomes like Jesus, who was stripped and made to suffer at the hands of his persecutors. Later in the story, Bem once again accepts his vulnerability to harm when he returns to his public persona. He knows and accepts the fact that in doing so he is deliberately drawing danger toward him. This, too, he receives as his opportunity to do God's will. Danger represents an opportunity for Bem and is therefore strangely freeing. The point is this: when we are in a position to will our own vulnerability, we can view potential harm as the source of potential benefit. Accepted vulnerability is quite different from forced. This is what makes a small group, for example, different from a gossip clique. Choosing to reveal one's vulnerabilities to a group is potentially empowering despite its risk because we can make the choice. The target of gossip has no such choice.

The vulnerability that comes with trusting, therefore, is not entirely negative. When we entrust ourselves or something we care about to another person, we do so because they can help us in a way that we cannot do by ourselves. Because we do not know how to do what they can do, we allow them a measure of discretion in how they take care of us. On a mundane level, Baier gives the example of entrusting a plumber to fix her drains. By definition, she cannot specify to the plumber the precise means by which she would like to have her drains cleared: "If I knew enough to compile [a list of means] I would myself have to be a competent plumber." She has to trust him to do a nonsubversive plumbing job, just as "he counts on me to do a nonsubversive teaching job, should he send his son to my course in the history of ethics."[21] To the plumber, the competing pedagogies for teaching ethics are as mysterious as drain-clearing methods are to Baier; each must allow the other latitude in their respective work, but each has a lot to gain by doing so.

At the same time, human vulnerability can become the thing that most challenges a trust relationship because vulnerability can cloud the very discernment the truster needs to exercise in order not to become a dupe. Vulnerability, in other words, puts us in a state where smart trust becomes more difficult. Relationships with professionals demonstrate this. As philosopher Edmund Pellegrino points out, we turn to professionals precisely for the help they can provide, but that also means we turn to them precisely when we are helpless.

> Trust is most problematic when we are in states of special dependency—in illness, old age, or infancy, or when we are in need of healing, justice, spiritual help, or learning. This is the situation in our relationships with the professions whom circumstances force us to trust. We are forced to trust professionals, if we wish access to their knowledge and skill. We need the help of doctors, lawyers, ministers, or teachers to surmount or cope with our most pressing human needs. We must depend on their fidelity to trust and their desire to protect, rather than exploit, our vulnerability.[22]

In other words, in the case of professional relationships, vulnerability is not only created when one person decides to trust another, but even predates the relationship. The truster comes already vulnerable and needy to this kind of trust relationship. Therefore, not only is the risk of harm from vulnerability even greater, but the truster is less able to choose their vulnerability. If accepted vulnerability to potential harm is nevertheless the hallmark of trust, somehow the client must maintain enough strength and independence from the professional to make judgments about the professional help they are receiving.

The ethics of clergy confidentiality must therefore recognize the vulnerability of the confider. People tell ministers precisely those things they feel unsafe telling others. They turn to the clergy at times of greatest insecurity and need. While we may eventually wish to critique a system whereby the clergyperson is the sole repository of all the community's anxiety and pain, we must nevertheless acknowledge that clergy often form deep trust relationships with people at the most vulnerable times in their lives. Mortality, guilt, despair, and other human conditions are the vulnerabilities clergy help others confront and make sense of. Put another way, the vulnerability of the human condition is precisely what makes the ethics of confidentiality challenging.

POWER

Because trusters are always put in some position of vulnerability vis-à-vis the people they entrust, the trust relationship always involves a differential of power. This is the third feature of trust we need to address. We tend not to think of trust in terms of power, one reason being that many trust relationships are mutual rather than unilateral. Friendship is a classic instance. Two friends often exchange information of an equally sensitive nature, both trusting the other to keep it confidential. In this case, neither has discernibly more power than the other so we do not notice any shift. But this does not mean that power is not involved; it is simply shared. If we were to take away the mutuality and substitute a pastor for the friend, we would immediately see the issue of power. Pastors' abuse of confidentiality is considered an abuse of their power.

Even in mutual relationships like friendship, however, we can detect the subtle play of power. As we will see in a later chapter, when gossip patterns among friends are studied, it is rare to find gossip being traded in precisely equal measure. Someone is always being talked about more than the rest. Certain members of the community also hear more gossip than the rest. Gossip, it turns out, proves to be a pretty reliable indicator of relative power within community. We need only extrapolate from friendship to congregational relationships to see that gossip is a force to be reckoned with inside the church. It is also a vehicle for distributing power. Those who can be safely entrusted with gossip are powerful individuals indeed, for they have a great deal of discretion at their disposal with respect to others' vulnerability. Those who indiscriminately talk about others behind their back, on the other hand, undermine trust within the community.

Discretionary power is by nature difficult to negotiate in advance. When I tell my secret to my small group, part of what I entrust them with is the freedom hereafter to use their judgment. Since I have trusted them, rather than made them sign a contract outlining the rules of confidentiality within our group (as I might with a therapist), I agree to extend them some latitude regarding the precise details of their actions. When I take my car in to my mechanic and entrust him with fixing the problems I have been experiencing when I drive, part of what I entrust him with is the freedom to repair parts that I did not even know were part of the problem. When I meet with my priest to discuss a spiritual matter, I do not get surprised if she inquires about other issues in my life, for I trust her to know something more than I do about the devices and desires of the human heart. In all these circumstances, I do not enter the relationship knowing everything that will transpire but allow someone else to exercise discretion in my life.

Because they are difficult to negotiate, the limits of discretionary power make all the difference. They become crucial to the ethics of trust as a practice. A smart truster will generally want to extend some, but not total, discretion. In Baier's terms, I may not wish to renounce full intelligence regarding appropriate uses of personal information, the inner workings of automobiles, or the yearnings of my soul. Attempting to communicate the appropriate limits of discretion, while still genuinely trusting the other, can be a very delicate interpersonal task. Spell out too many details and you effectively kill the trust, but hand over completely free reign and you risk becoming even more vulnerable. Power balances are not only difficult to broker initially but also to maintain.

The issue of power, after all, does not get settled with the initial act of entrusting. If anything, it becomes more complicated as the entrusted party starts to exercise discretion and the truster responds. Either party to the trust relationship can affect it down the road. The person entrusted with something valuable might over time become careless or forgetful. But so also the truster might jump too quickly to conclusions about what constitutes carelessness. She might react too hastily to perceived abuses of trust, leading the entrusted person to become resentful, and possibly even less trustworthy. Baier wisely notes: "One thing that can destroy a trust relationship fairly quickly is the combination of a rigorous unforgiving attitude on the part of the truster and a touchy sensitivity to any criticism on the part of the trusted."[23]

Good trust relationships, in other words, require judicious and ongoing exercise of judgment on the part of everyone involved. This keeps power in check. My small group partners might have to judge whether my best interest would actually be served by revealing my secret to someone outside the group. If they were to reveal it, I would have to judge whether they genuinely had my interests at heart or simply gave in to the temptation of gossip (a very difficult judgment to make when a community confuses pastoral care and gossip, as so many do). Nor do failures of trust always remand to the entrusted. Failure on the part of the truster to forgive a relatively minor abuse of discretionary power is also a way to break it. If I turn accusingly on my small group because they want to seek our pastor's counsel even though this is technically against "the rules," it could be argued that I am not a very good truster.

It can be tempting not to do the work. Too often when the delicacy and difficulty of these judgments settle in or when we get stung by one too many breaches of trust, we jettison trust and go in search of surer, more reliable ways to ensure the well-being of the things we care about. This happens all the time in individual and communal life. Typically the turn is toward formalization, that is, people seeking to establish a formal relationship rather than the trust relationship they currently have. Often they seek a contractual relationship. Examples run from the mundane to the serious. The departmental staff members who have always implicitly trusted each other to cover each other's areas insist on more precise, written job descriptions once some are perceived to slack off. The plumber who used to proceed with work on the basis of a verbal agreement alone now demands a signed acceptance of his estimate. Parents in a church who have always left their children in the care of others start asking for background checks. The harder path to take is attempting to sustain trust without all the formal systems and structures and rules.

Formal arrangements are especially difficult to resist in situations of obviously unequal power. Low-wage workers, for example, can only trust so long in the company's good name before they rightly worry that their jobs may be outsourced and decide to seek a contract guaranteeing job security. The stay-at-home mother divorcing a wealthy man may not forever be able to trust him to support their children but probably instead needs a binding agreement. (Infants left in the care of an ever-changing roster of unskilled nursery assistants probably represent a powerless group in need of protection.) Nor should formalities necessarily be resisted. Less powerful individuals need and deserve the assurance that contracts and rules provide. My point, therefore, is not that the oppressed and powerless ought to be more trusting. That would resolve little. My point is this: not every situation *can* be formalized, nor can contract alone solve every problem. At some point, trust is still indispensable in human interactions. Even unions have to strive for trust between workers and management. Even divorced parents have to entrust each other with certain aspects of their children's well-being. The moment of trust arrives, as I have explained, when we are forced to act despite not having all the confidence we might like, nor all the information at hand, nor all the details fully spelled out. And that moment inevitably arrives in any meaningful relationship. We do ourselves a disservice if we think that all relationships can be covered by contract. We will always need to figure out who is worthy of our trust. We will always have to take some risks with those with whom we interact.

We cannot always stipulate forever what others should do with the things we care about.[24]

Those in positions of relatively unequal power need not feel that they must "throw themselves back on" trust. As I hope I have made clear, trust is not the same thing as blind reliance. Conditions can be created that nurture and support it. One of the most important conditions is transparency. When we find ourselves in a position where we have to trust others (like ministers) who have more power over us, we need to be able to articulate to ourselves and to them what we are entrusting, and why. Baier called this the "expressibility test" for trust. If I am about to trust you, I ought to be in a position to tell you what risk I am taking, how you can make me vulnerable, and even what power over me you might come to have if our trust relationship goes forward. The sheer ability to make transparent the risk of trusting, in other words, itself softens it.

Perhaps the best way to understand the expressibility test is to imagine a trust relationship that fails it. Let me paraphrase an example I have used elsewhere.

> If I entrust my small group with a secret only because I know they lack the comprehension to understand it and would be too embarrassed to admit so, I am relying on their incomprehension and their pride. Probably I will not express this reason; I can hardly tell them that I am relying on their incomprehension! They, in turn, will not be in any position to refuse the confidence because they will be embarrassed to admit they do not understand the secret. I have, in effect, coerced their trust because I did not express its terms. The situation makes us all vulnerable (the group perhaps more than me), but none of us can name the vulnerability. We cannot talk about it.[25]

In a trust relationship, all parties ought to be able to name the risk, vulnerability, and power involved.

Philosopher Onora O'Neill puts it another way. She describes the trust relationship as a relationship of accountability.[26] When we trust people who have power over us, we are not in a position to control what they might do, but we can nevertheless find ways to hold them accountable to us. Someone is properly accountable to us when we can make an informed, independent, and intelligible decision about what they are doing. (These are the three *I*s of trust, according to O'Neill.) She has in mind professionals like journalists, whose handling of the truth it is very difficult for many of us to assess and who thus exercise a good deal of power over us by what they write and say. As consumers of journalism, most readers and listeners cannot know the sources being cited or the accuracy of the claims being made. Nevertheless, our judgments about the content of the news can still be more or less informed, independent, and intelligible. If we know that a news organization, for example, is owned by a particular corporation, then we can make a more informed decision about their reporting on that corporation's actions than if we were kept in the dark. If we have access to multiple rather than singular sources of news, we can make independent judgments about the biases and accuracy of each. If the news content is reported and interpreted in terms we can understand and is not made overly complex or technical, then we can render intelligible judgments about it.

Although she does not use the same terms, what O'Neill effectively recommends is that in keeping professionals accountable to the rest of us, we must acknowledge the power they have over us and the vulnerability of being under their sway, and then we must seek to minimize that vulnerability by strengthening our own ability to judge their actions as best we can.

Supporters in the wider community also play a role by keeping an eye on trust relationships of unequal power. It is not unusual for trusters and entrusted alike to need the help of others, if only their watchful presence. By this I do not necessarily mean inspections and tests by third parties to the trust relationship. I mean, rather, the witness of others to the trust we have given and received and the wisdom of others regarding its perpetuation. Others can remind us of the initial reasons for our trusting (or not trusting). They can gently point out to us the breaches of trust we are unwilling to see (or the fidelity we are too grudging to acknowledge). They are often better than us at discerning when the terms of the trust relationship no longer match the worth of Valued Thing C or recognizing when, in order to keep C safe, the terms should change. Others also help us immensely through their own good examples. A community that practices trust well sets the standard time and again until well-practiced trust comes to seem the norm.

Finally, those with less power can decide to blend trust with some form of contract. After all, the two options are not exclusive. Even trust, though stronger than mere reliance, is not always the best choice. Sometimes, when power is entrenched and uneven, the better part of wisdom suggests healthy distrust rather than trust. We can and should form a variety of kinds of relationships in our communities, depending on the flow of power within them, and contractual relationships have their proper place. As we will see, this holds true even in churches.

THE ETHICS OF TRUST RELATIONSHIPS

In a lecture on trust delivered in 2006, theologian Jürgen Moltmann quoted the famous line of Lenin: "Trust is good but control is better." The aim of Moltmann's lecture was to argue the opposite: while control may be good, trust is better.[27] In many cases I would affirm that trust is indeed better and, I would additionally argue, more sophisticated morally. In a Christian context, given trust's resemblance to faith, it could be argued that as people of faith we are always called to be trusting. I would affirm that trust relationships are rich and meaningful and generally good for us to form. At the same time, however, there are many ordinary circumstances in life where it would undoubtedly be better if we knew what was going to happen and did not have to go out on a limb! As I have just finished arguing, control is not necessarily a bad thing. Therefore, the above conversation about trust was meant to be a description, not a prescription. We are not always meant to entrust our "valuables" to others. It simply is the case that sometimes we have to.

And when we have to trust others, we should do so with wisdom and care. While we may not be able to affirm that trust is always better than control, we can surely say that there are better and worse forms of trust (not to mention control). The ethics of trust that I propose may be summarized in three prescriptive statements related to the three features of trust I have elaborated—risk, vulnerability, and power. First, any risk taken by truster or entrusted must be reasonable; that is, it must be proportional to the valued thing being entrusted. Most of the time, we have the truster in mind here, for they take a risk in entrusting themselves. But as we shall see in the next chapter, sometimes those entrusted with valuable things take risks as well. Second, any vulnerability must be accepted by the truster. Third, any power differential between truster and trusted must be minimized. If these three "prescriptions" for trust can be met, then the trust relationship is most likely a morally sound one. If they cannot, trust is inadvisable.

Let me relate these prescriptive statements to the Prisoners' Dilemma by way of concluding this chapter. Fascinated by the challenge to human behavior this game represented, theorists during the 1980s tried to figure out what strategy would guarantee a winning score if the game were played repeatedly. If you played round after round, would it make sense to defect often, hoping to lower your opponent's score and increase your own, or instead take a chance on cooperation, keeping your own score lower but ensuring a closer contest? Computer models were designed to discern the winningest strategy.

It turned out that being "greedy," that is, frequently defecting on one's partner, was shown to be an unsuccessful strategy. In the long run, it was better to risk cooperation. However, consistently cooperating, no matter what choice your partner made, was not a wise strategy either. As it turns out, the best strategy for winning at the Prisoner's Dilemma appeared to be what was rather humbly called "Tit for Tat": to win, do whatever your partner just did. Giving tit for tat may not seem like a terribly sophisticated strategy for the moral life, but the analogy is apt nonetheless, and it captures our first prescription for healthy trust. In trust relationships, it is important that Person A not take a disproportionately greater risk than Person B. Their risk should also remain in proportion to the value of what they hope to keep safe.

Computer models of the Prisoner's Dilemma additionally revealed that it was a good idea occasionally to forgive, that is, to cooperate even if your partner just defected on you. To us, this suggests that something can be gained from making oneself vulnerable. Any vulnerability, however, should be freely chosen as much as possible or else the trusting person simply becomes a dupe, exposing herself unnecessarily to harm and loss. This is our second prescription for trust.

In the end, the computers generated four rules for maximizing one's success in the face of this kind of trust dilemma.[28] Put simply, the rules were:

1. Be nice.
2. Retaliate if necessary.
3. Occasionally forgive.
4. Don't be envious.

In the terms of the Prisoner's Dilemma, "be nice" means generally following a pattern of cooperation rather than defection. "Retaliate if necessary" means defecting on a tit-for-tat basis. "Occasionally forgiving" translates into resuming your cooperative pattern even when defected upon, and steadfastly choosing cooperation even though it keeps you from achieving a high score is what it means not to be "envious."

For our purposes, these four rules reinforce our prescriptions for trust relationships. "Being nice" translates into a willingness to risk entrusting others and building a relationship with them. It also means that if you are Person B, you should not harm Person A who is trusting you. You should not force them to take risks that will render them inordinately vulnerable to harm. You should not be quirky and unpredictable with how you treat their Valued Thing C, for this puts them on the defensive, strains the trust relationship you have established, and does not grow the trust between you. On the other hand, "retaliate if necessary" means that if you are Person A, you should never put yourself at risk of *too* much harm. If Person B becomes untrustworthy, you do not have to continue to go along. Trust relationships do not benefit from one person being a pushover or blind optimist. "Occasionally forgive" means accepting vulnerability but also taking a gentle approach to minor breaches of trust. As Annette Baier puts it, trusters have to decide whether "the best response is indignant complaint and unforgiving withdrawal of trust, or whether apologies and new starts are acceptable."[29] Finally, "don't be envious" speaks to the attitude between truster and entrusted. If either party tries too hard to "score points" in the trust relationship, the relationship will be unsound. Genuine trust requires what Margaret Farley calls a "relaxation of heart,"[30] a charitable and nonanxious attitude toward the other. Those who seek to increase their power advantage, as we have seen, do little to advance trust. Our third prescription affirms that trust is most successfully maintained when neither party has cause to be fearful or jealous of the other's power but, rather, when power between the two is balanced.

CONCLUSION

In closing, then, let us bring Cardinal Bem back to mind. It could be said that Bem first understands trust as a practice when he understands its opposite—mistrust. When he is being held captive by forces he still believes may be the Security Police, he becomes aware of the practiced authority with which the "colonel" suspects insurrection. Listening to this man, Bem realizes that the colonel's sense of what is going on has not been gathered by accident. Rather, "he bathes daily in a running tap of words inspired by fear and greed, in secret reports of unwary talk, in denunciations inspired by hatred, words spoken after torture." The colonel and his forces are expert in the ways of mistrust: forcing information out of people, issuing ultimatums, feeding hate. They deal all the time in trickery, torture, and subterfuge. Mistrust is their life. They "bathe daily" in it. With a sinking heart, Bem further realizes that the church's power is no match for this expertise. "It is the state's business to know these things. The church has no comparable intelligence." What Bem eventually learns, of course, is that while the church may have no comparable system for ferreting out political information, it is practiced in following another truth. What "intelligence" the church has is not the fruit of secrecy and fear. It is the fruit of trusting relationships, carefully developed and attended to over time and relying always on God's grace to overcome human fallibility. If the church is to exercise power and wisdom, it will be through steadfast commitment to *this* practice.

Chapter Two

✺ CONFIDENTIALITY

In the last chapter we used a fictional character, Cardinal Bem, to illustrate how someone learns a better, smarter way to practice trust in others. The cardinal's education in trust came at the expense of having to endure some extraordinary, horrible situations where he found it nearly impossible to entrust himself to anybody. Naturally, we would not wish such an education on anyone! But his story nevertheless imparts some important lessons about ordinary, everyday trust: that if it is taken for granted it will probably not last long; that forging nonsuperficial trust relationships requires taking risk and accepting vulnerability; and that at the same time, such relationships demand a certain amount of shrewdness and even calculation. Appropriate, healthy trust also involves a careful reading of the balance of power between truster and entrusted and an effort to ensure that in handing over something to another, one is giving away neither too much nor too little. Trust, in short, is never easy.

In the remaining chapters of this book, we will consider several relational practices that people in the church have a tendency to make easy. They are problematic because relationships built on shortcuts will ultimately undermine the flourishing of trust in the church. So-called safe church measures are an attempt to lock in trust relationships through a bureaucracy of formal rules and regulations; ironically, these attempts at behavior control too often lull people into thinking they have done "enough" in the way of trusting each other. Gossip, itself an *easy* way that people talk to one another, is either discounted as unimportant or embraced too readily as a form of "pastoral care." Bullshit, a form of communicating that offers style when substance is wanted, confuses those who are gullible

and alienates those who see through it. In the current chapter, we take up
the practice of keeping secrets that we call confidentiality. People in the
church have sometimes attempted to make confidentiality easy by adopting a blanket rule whereby clergy must keep silent about everything they
hear. Like any attempt to solve a moral problem too easily, this solution
has not always worked. Neither, however, would its opposite—the sharing
of all information publicly. I will attempt to shed light on the dilemmas
surrounding confidentiality by taking secret information to be the "valued
thing" that one person entrusts to another and applying the lessons we
have learned about what sustains good trust relationships.

It has been pointed out that the etymology of the word *confide* is the
combination of the Latin prefix "with" and the verb "trust" (*com-* and
fidere). As one writer puts it, "Therefore, at its root, *confide* conveys a sense
of sharing something *with trust* or *with faith*. In fact the English word *to
entrust* may be a close synonym to the verb *to confide*. . . . To confide* is to
place in trust and the one who receives the confidence becomes a stew-
ard or trustee."[1] Confidences are literally a matter of trust! It is therefore
appropriate to treat confidentiality as an example of entrusting. The things
we say when we confide in others are like possessions we give to another for
safekeeping. All the same issues of risk, vulnerability, and power associated
with the trust relationship apply also to confidentiality.

What are some of the dilemmas of clergy confidentiality? Clergy frequently face the struggle between saying too little and saying too much.
They feel bound (at least initially) by an ethic of total silence, which would
ostensibly oblige them not to repeat what they heard no matter when and
where they heard it. At the same time, we know that laypeople routinely
expect clergy to divulge information. They want their pastor to serve as a
sort of central clearinghouse of information for the community. Pastors
report, for example, that frequently when talking with a group of parishioners one will inquire, "How is Mrs. X doing after her operation?," assuming that they can make public the details of Mrs. X's condition. Situations
like this put clergy in a difficult spot: to repeat what they think is casual
information for a wide audience and risk breaking the confider's trust or
to withhold information they deem private and risk alienating those who
consider themselves part of the confider's caring community. These con-
flicting expectations laid on clergy regarding confidentiality can be confus-
ing because it seems they are likely to break trust no matter what they do.

Another dilemma arises when clergy have to decide how much
information a third party needs. In these cases their role is not so much

clearinghouse but mediator. An example might be ministers serving on a committee that endorses and disciplines others engaged in ministry. They know things that congregations might benefit from knowing. Or field educators in theological schools, who often have to decide how much to tell a mentor about their seminarian, or vice versa. Clergy playing a mediating role may believe that by intervening with what they know they will be able to help create deeper relationships or reconcile difficult ones. If they choose to intervene, however, they run the risk of disrespecting someone's privacy or, perhaps worse, cutting off the trust that could have grown between groups or individuals if they had had the courage to work on their relationship themselves.

Clergy occasionally face quite grave confidentiality situations as well. Some have become embroiled in conflicts that are taken to court. An attorney in one U.S. denomination recently predicted that confidentiality would be the next big legal issue on the horizon in parish ministry.[2] This is because clergy become privy to sensitive information that third parties claim to have a right to know. Take, for example, a parishioner who confesses thoughts, or even plans, of suicide but begs her pastor not to tell her family. Consider the youth group members who tell the seminary intern about an abusive teenager that their parents know nothing about. Cases like these put pressure on clergy to alert somebody else about what they know.

These are just some of the dilemmas of clergy confidentiality, of which we will consider more later in the chapter. Clergy also face cases that are *not* in fact dilemmas but that people try to make into ones. Even this very brief review of confidentiality cases makes clear that "Clergy should keep silent everything they hear" is an overly simplistic ethic. Several attempts by ethicists to apply principles like fidelity and justice fare better, but these too have their limits. I will hope to show that an ethic of trust is best of all. In general, I will be arguing that confidentiality would best promote trust relationships in the church if clergy confidences were carefully honored once accepted, but accepted more sparingly.[3]

First, however, it will help to define terms as I am going to use them. When one person entrusts another with information, and asks that it be kept secret, I call this a "confidence." The person telling the secret is a confider, and the person hearing the secret a confidant. The act of keeping the information secret I call "confidentiality." In other words, by confidentiality I mean secret keeping with a promise attached. The promise may or may not be explicit (this is often where the problems arise) but strictly speaking, a confidence implies a promise, and this is what distinguishes it from other forms of information sharing. Promising is what seals the confider and confidant in a trust relationship. There are a great many other instances of secrecy—defined simply as any form of concealment—that do not come under the heading of confidentiality because a promissory relationship between people is not explicitly invoked. (One example might be the secret passwords we increasingly use today in online transactions.) There are also ways we obtain secret information about others, like through gossip or the grapevine, that do not necessarily count as confidences even if we keep them to ourselves.

I should also note up front that I do not take secret keeping to be either a bad or a good thing in and of itself. There are some who attach a negative connotation to the word *secrecy* and are therefore willing to embrace ministerial confidentiality (which has honorable connotations) but not secrecy. A denominational paper on confidentiality, for instance, distinguishes it from secrecy by associating the latter with "competition and distrust" and, further, by making secrecy into a moral absolute and confidentiality a negotiable matter:

> Secrets involve the mutual agreement among all participants that the secret will not be disclosed under any circumstances, at any time, with any person not also sworn to maintain the secret. Secrets may only be divulged upon the dissolution of the secrecy agreement or when a person is released from the oath of secrecy.

In contrast:

> Confidences are not secrets, but are always shared with the understanding that they will be shared as appropriate in order to foster and promote the interests and well being of the confider.[4]

I do not believe such a liberal understanding of confidence sharing exists in popular opinion; I think that—for better or worse—most of us believe confidences *are* secrets. Therefore, I do not draw this kind of distinction between secrecy and confidentiality. It seems to me wiser to treat confidences as secrets, and then engage the moral questions of which ones to accept and under which circumstances their disclosure might be warranted. Eventually I may wish to agree that confider and confidant should approach confidences with the sort of understanding described here, but

I see no particular advantage to defining secrecy in negative or absolute terms. Keeping a confidence is keeping a secret, and even if you are not agreeing to hold onto anything wrong, by becoming a confidant you *are* engaging in secrecy as opposed to openness. In addition, I wish to treat confidentiality the way I do trust—as something generally to be recommended in human life but always worth pausing to question. Some confidences should not be kept. Therefore, I will not assume that agreeing to keep a confidence is necessarily always better than declining.

Most of the time there are perfectly justifiable and innocent reasons not to make information open to others, but occasionally the reasons become dubious. Those are precisely the situations that give pause and that we will wish to examine in this chapter. When is confidentiality requested or accepted in order to strengthen a trust relationship, and when are there other intentions? We wish not simply to ask when a clergyperson ought to keep or break confidentiality but to take a slightly different approach and ask how clergy can use confidentiality to grow trust within their communities.

POPULAR ASSUMPTIONS ABOUT CLERGY CONFIDENTIALITY

I have stated that many church folk think that clergy must keep silent about everything they hear. This popular assumption—what ministry ethicist Joseph Bush calls "the popular perspective's elevation of confidentiality"[5]—has found support in the literature on the topic. One 1994 essay on the professional ethics of confidentiality includes a chart correlating various professions with the subject matters that can be kept confidential within them. It says that lawyers, for example, can keep everything their clients tell them secret except for information concerning future criminal activity; that information they must divulge. The ministry is unique among the chart's professions for lacking any subject matter that clergy are required to divulge. The chart simply reads: "Cleric——All information."[6] As many of us know, laws have recently been revised on this matter and in most states, clergy must now divulge information about child abuse or neglect. They are included among the list of "mandated reporters" identified by states as persons who by virtue of their occupation must report knowledge of such cases. However, popular perception persists in the view that clergy are persons to whom the right to silence is extended nearly absolutely.

In 1998, Congregational pastor D. Elizabeth Audette reported on the results of a survey she had conducted among three hundred ministers and laypeople in her denomination in an article for *The Christian Century*. Her findings revealed some interesting assumptions about clergy confidentiality. For example, "most of those surveyed assumed that anything told to a clergyperson anywhere should be treated confidentially, regardless of the circumstances of the disclosure."[7] Her work confirmed the idea that assumptions about confidentiality were attached to the role or identity of the ordained clergyperson, for survey respondents did not apply the same reasoning to laypeople, even if they were church leaders. In addition, fellow members of the church should be no more privy to the information told a clergyperson, they said, than "a person on the street."[8]

What has influenced popular perception on this matter? As Bush points out, at least two factors are probably in play.[9] First, many people instinctively compare ministry to medicine and other health-care fields, and simply conflate ministers with those who should follow a rule of practitioner-patient confidentiality. And so one author wrote several years ago, "Pastors, like physicians, assume a lifelong, broad, interpersonal, and familial responsibility for persons. Thus, they should treat all that they hear as confidential, because by divulging it they may endanger or make more difficult the lives of those entrusted to their care."[10] Indeed, Audette found that most respondents to her survey viewed ministers the way they did therapists. (This was true of both clergy and lay respondents.) It followed that they regarded the clergyperson's responsibility the same way they did a secular therapist's, namely, the strict keeping of all confidences. As Audette put it, "Their views were informed by a therapeutic model. . . . Confidentiality, then, became a matter of professional (counseling) ethics."[11] Her respondents did not articulate a difference between secular and ecclesial settings nor did they offer any theological rationales for an ethic of confidentiality.

Interestingly, however, Audette's respondents did identify one difference between their assumptions about clergy versus secular therapists. Most of them thought that clergy were supposed to keep all secrets no matter how they came by the information, assuming, as we have heard, that clergy should keep confidences "regardless of the circumstances of the disclosure." Presumably, those circumstances included everything from chance encounters in the grocery store to scheduled appointments in the pastor's office.[12] Even a family physician might not be held to the same expectation. If Audette's respondents are representative of many in the church, therefore, we have a potential contradiction at work in many people's minds: on the one hand, church folk consider clergy no different from other professionals with regard to confidentiality, but on the other hand, they still treat clergy as a special class of professional who, by virtue of their calling, are supposed to keep nearly all information confidential.

The second influence upon popular perception is the trope of the confessional booth: the idea that clergy and parishioners occupy a space where all is kept sacrosanct. Many assume that all clergy, regardless of denomination or tradition, are allowed to keep absolute silence the way Roman Catholic priests under the seal of the confessional are. But even a court of law will look to the practices followed within a particular denomination before granting clergy a right to silence. A clergyperson can only claim confidentiality if information was obtained in the practice of conducting a legitimately recognized sacrament of confession. (Even then, actual practice will vary from court to court.) This is related to a third influence, that of the notion of privileged communication. Privilege is a legal protection extended by the courts to persons in certain carefully defined relationships, exempting them from testifying in court. Many believe that clergy will always be granted privilege in relationship to their parishioners, but actual practice does not support this perception.[13]

Clergy sometimes seem loath to correct popular perception on clergy confidentiality. As Bush writes, "That [pastoral confidence is held absolutely] is actually a misperception is frequently left uncorrected by clergy in their encounters with others."[14] Furthermore, denominational practices around ordination underscore the sacredness of confidentiality and seem to suggest it is absolute. In my own denomination, the United Church of Christ, one of the vows taken by ordinands in the ordination service is "Will you keep silent all confidences shared with you?"[15]

PRACTICES OF CONFIDENTIALITY

One result of popular perceptions about clergy confidentiality, I believe, is that too many members of Christians congregations have lost the ability to entrust *each other* with sensitive information. People will turn to their pastors, chaplains, and other religious professionals but not to their community. Too few communities of faith today bear any resemblance to the relational practices of congregational life prescribed in the letter to James: "Are any among you suffering? They should pray. Are any cheerful? They should sing songs of praise. Are any among you sick? They should call for the elders of the church and have them pray over them, anointing them with oil in the name of the Lord. The power of the faith will save the sick, and the Lord will raise them up; and anyone who has committed sins will be forgiven. *Therefore confess your sins to one another, and pray for one another,* so that you may be healed" (4:13-16, emphasis added). Church folk today may be reasonably capable of rejoicing in each other's lives and praying for each other's illnesses, but do we find many fellowships where sufferings and failings are revealed in any deep and genuine way? Instances of public revelation may *appear* to abound today, especially among famous church leaders who are treated like celebrities when they come clean to their congregations about past misdeeds, but these desperate rituals are more like deathbed confessions of the Middle Ages than they are a model for ordinary church practice. One can only make such a dramatic appeal for forgiveness once in a lifetime, after all. The popularity of these celebrated tell-all events belies the real situation in everyday churches. Most of us are not baring our souls publicly nor, I suspect, would most of our communities tolerate it. If there are many congregations where self-revelation is meaningfully practiced, they would seem to be few and far between.

In 1938, Dietrich Bonhoeffer wrote a little book called *Life Together* that captures with remarkable insight the realities of ordinary Christian community. Decades later, his words still ring true. Bonhoeffer, of course, was a German theologian who joined the resistance against his country's Nazi regime. Christians who refused to seek refuge in other countries but who also refused to cooperate with the German government were called the Confessing Church. They had to operate in a clandestine manner and even then, many, including Bonhoeffer, were eventually arrested and put to death. *Life Together* was inspired by the community of twenty-five religious men who lived together during the late 1930s in a sort of underground seminary. Despite the extraordinary circumstances about and under which Bonhoeffer was writing, however, his description of Christian community is amazingly mundane. He constantly reminds his reader that even at its best, real Christian life together is a struggle. In particular, he reflects on the ways that Christians exhibit false piety when it comes to divulging our sin. We put up fronts when it comes to admitting the true state of our souls. Writing with a degree of sarcasm, he says, "The pious fellowship permits no one to be a sinner. So everyone must conceal his sin from himself and from the fellowship." This prevents the "final break-through to fellowship" from occurring because "though they have fellowship with one another as believers and as devout people, they do not have fellowship as the undevout, as sinners."[16]

Bonhoeffer therefore appealed to his brothers, and his readers, to find the courage to confess their secrets to one another and thereby discover true community in Christ. He cited New Testament practices of sharing confidences within the community by suggesting that a sinner could make confession to anyone. "According to Jesus' promise, every Christian brother can hear the confession of another."[17] Incidentally, Bonhoeffer was eminently realistic and did not deem it necessary to confide in the *entire* community. One member could stand in for the rest: "I meet the whole community in the one brother to whom I confess my sins and who forgives my sins."[18] He also took pains to emphasize that no single member of the community should hear all the community's confessions. "It is not a good thing," he said simply, "for one person to be the confessor for all the others."[19] Bonhoeffer's appeal bears repeating today. Many of us hide our problems and masquerade as people who have it all together spiritually, achieving fellowship only "as believers and as devout people." We hesitate to entrust ourselves to one another.

The remaining exception, of course, appears to be the pastor's office. There, people often feel free to unburden themselves—supported, perhaps by their perceptions of the pastor's inviolable silence. Many people will go to talk to the pastor before they will talk to anyone else in church about the problems in their lives. But this tendency to lay everything on the pastor is worth critiquing.

I hasten to say that pastors clearly have a unique and important professional role in counseling parishioners. People need someone to whom they can take their deepest problems and concerns. As pointed out in chapter 1, part of what it means to be a professional is to receive people in their most vulnerable state. Therefore, there is no substitute for someone who can remain steady and supportive in the face of vulnerability. In the church, this is what pastors do for us. When we are most needy and conflicted, it is risky for us to bare our souls, and we cannot and should not be expected to bare them to just anyone. It will always be important to have someone within the community who exercises the special competencies of listening, comforting, and providing counsel. In other words, there is no denying the irreplaceable role that clergy play in hearing confessions and other confidences.

What I am arguing is that there may be cases in which there are other venues besides the pastor's office for talking about the problems that burden us. Theologian William Willimon made this point several years ago when he gave the example of the parishioner who confided in him that her son was an alcoholic. She asked that he not share this information with anyone in the congregation, for fear they would think less of her. His reaction:

> I have two problems with her request. First, two-thirds of the congregation already know her son is an alcoholic. A congregation that doesn't know intimate information about one another isn't much of a church. Second, the dozen or so members of the church who are parents of alcoholic children could be her primary path to care. As her pastor, I must help her to see that her deep, unmentionable secret is in the eyes of faith a church problem. . . . [20]

Pastors need not be the only avenue for pastoral care. Willimon puts it even more pointedly:

> Indeed, I've decided that one of the greatest and most indefensible burdens pastors bear is knowing so many secrets about their parishioners. Why should the pastor be expected to be the sole repository of other people's pain? We need to re-examine the whole notion of privacy and confidentiality in ministry.[21]

Willimon has great faith in the church as a community where people can safely risk telling their secrets. He may in fact at times be guilty of overestimating the trust level that exists in typical congregations. (I, for one, am certainly aware of congregations where the members don't necessarily "know intimate information about one another" and where a mother would feel lucky if two-thirds of the congregation knew *her*, let alone her son's alcoholism.) But his point is still well taken and his description of the pastor as "repository" challenges us to reconsider the role of the pastor in the hearing of confidences. Might it not also be the role of clergy to encourage the airing of more information within the community? Could they not play a more active role in making the unmentionable mentionable? Could clergy give up their "privileged" position in favor of helping to grow trust between others by getting them to talk more openly and freely to each other?

THE INFLUENCE OF THE THERAPEUTIC

Let us take up Willimon's challenge and reexamine, for a moment, the notion of confidentiality. I think we need to be clearer about the fact that the ministry both is and is not like other professions, for this is where some of the moral tensions lie with respect to how clergy are supposed to relate to people in their care. As both formal surveys and anecdotal evidence suggest, we hold clergy almost to a double standard, expecting them to act simultaneously like therapists to individuals and like shepherds to "flocks." Therefore, we cannot treat the ethics of clergy confidentiality as simply continuous with the ethics of other professions, applying principles that have been generated for doctors and lawyers, and so on, who care for individuals but do not necessarily lead communities.

It is hard to underestimate the contemporary influence on ministry of what Audette calls the "therapeutic model." Indeed, I would argue that a significant part of our problem, when it comes to the ethics of confidentiality, is that the ministry is no longer distinguishable from secular professions like psychotherapy. These, after all, are founded on the therapeutic need for strict professional-client confidentiality. In the therapeutic relationship, confidentiality serves to establish a safe space within which disclosures can be made. Treatment depends on the successful establishment of this space. This logic goes like this: an assurance of a confidential environment lets the client build a special relationship with the therapist, and this relationship is in turn what helps the client make discoveries and disclosures and eventually, progress in their treatment. In other words, the professional-client trust relationship is considered a crucial condition for therapeutic effectiveness, and must be maintained through promises of confidentiality. Were a therapist to broadcast details about a client, this would sever their relationship and she would never see her client again. Confidentiality facilitates the work being done.

Why should the ministry be any different? Clergy have applied the same logic to the pastoral care and counseling they do. They, too, define trustworthiness in terms of keeping parishioners' confidences. They, too, assume that sharing information about parishioners will kill the relationship they have built and represent a violation of their pastoral role. Clergy may use different moral language than that used by other professionals, but the basic logic is often the same: in relationship to the clergyperson, the confider must enjoy the safety of knowing that what she says will not be disclosed.

Others writing on ministry ethics seek to draw the same parallels between the ministry and therapeutic professions. Take, for example, Richard Gula's ethic of confidentiality. A Roman Catholic moral theologian, Gula wrote a book called *Ethics in Pastoral Ministry* as a way to "apply to pastoral ministry some of the work being done in professional ethics."[22] He rests his ethic upon a foundation of three covenantal virtues—fidelity, justice, and prudence. Fidelity is, for him, the one most relevant to matters of trust like confidentiality. It is what keeps the relationship between pastor and parishioner intact. "Fidelity, or trustworthiness, is the covenantal virtue required to maintain the bonds of the pastoral relationship."[23] Justice, on the other hand, is the virtue clergy call upon when keeping a confidence poses a threat of harm to the parishioner or someone else. "If fidelity is the covenantal virtue that we need in order to maintain the bonds that we make with the one seeking the pastoral service, then justice is the virtue that recognizes our interdependence with all people."[24] In a case whereby the threat is too great, an appeal to justice allows a priest to disclose information. To put it simply, the virtue of justice in such a case trumps the virtue of fidelity. The logic is similar to that established for the therapy world: confidentiality is a *prima facie* duty that professionals may nevertheless set aside, on rare occasion, to protect an innocent, outside third party from harm.

It is typical of the field of professional ethics to pose the moral problem this way. The trust of the individual to whom a fiduciary duty is owed is set in potential opposition to the good of the larger community. One encyclopedia entry on confidentiality even describes the individual as "pitted against" the rest of society: "The most common objective justifying infringement of confidentiality is that of preventing harm or not causing harm. Thus, the interests of clients/patients/penitents to whom the professional owes the *prima facie* duty of confidentiality are pitted against the interests of others in society (or society itself) who may be harmed if the professional secret is kept."[25] It may be the case that preventing or not causing harm, if broadly defined, is the most common reason for breaking a confidence one has agreed to keep. I myself have argued that trust relationships often snap under the strain of all the vulnerability they are asked to bear. But affirming this as a common justification for breaches of confidentiality does not mean that the danger of such breaches is frequently faced. The duty-to-individuals-versus-harm-to-society dilemma is so central to the professional ethics literature as to make one think that clergy and other professionals face it on a regular basis. I am not sure this is accurate. It seems to me that other sorts of dilemmas, like what counts as a reasonable confidence in the first place, crop up in ministry practice just as often if not more. A Lutheran writer commenting on confidentiality issues in the ministry was honest about the infrequency with which pastors risk harm by keeping dangerous secrets. On the ground, this supposedly classic problem in the professional ethics literature just does not happen very often: "When a parishioner shares in private confession or confidential communication, it must not be disclosed. If a person is in danger of harming himself/herself or another person, there are exceptions about disclosure. However, these are rare and not common."[26]

What is wrong with borrowing the ethics of a secular profession? There are several problems as I see it. First, therapy is based on a closed, one-on-one relationship between a professional and a client. Therapists and clients see each other in privacy, typically in the therapist's office, and neither expects interaction outside of that private space. As Audette puts it, secular counselors "see clients in well-defined professional settings."[27] We have already pointed out the dissimilarity here to the ministry. Therapists and clients, second, do not typically have other connections. In fact, clients often deliberately choose therapists who do not belong to their social and professional circles. This is not just to avoid conflict of interest but also to enhance their privacy. What this means is that the two are not together part of a network of other relationships. Let me state the obvious: a professional presumably has relationships with many other clients and the client with many other people besides the therapist, but these additional people are not party to the therapeutic relationship. The boundaries of the therapeutic relationship are drawn around just two people, therapist and client. Their relationship does not belong to a wider set of communal relationships. There is no community.

In contrast, the church *is* a community. It includes members who enjoy various levels of relationship with one another. They know one another, at least as fellow communicants, they interact, and they relate to one another as people mutually bound in fellowship. They can never get completely away from each other. Church members understand that their community is built on "ties that bind" them to each other. They all individually and collectively relate to God in Christ. Many metaphors for the church show forth this understanding, most notably the metaphor of church as the body of Christ. The clergyperson, though to a degree set apart from the rest of the body (depending on theology), is still a member of it. Her calling is to serve the whole body *and* to serve the individual members of it. Therefore, her relationships with individual members can never be entirely closed, for they are always situated within the context of the wider body from which they draw their meaning and strength. Any individual relationships that laypeople have with the clergy—and, for that matter, with each other—are encompassed by the relationship they have to the whole community and to God.

Both/and relationships characterize other faith communities besides congregations. In the first chapter, we used the case of a small group as an example of a trust relationship. Members of such groups have special ties that bind them in a circle, but they also still belong to the congregation at large. In educational institutions, the chaplains and administrators and professors relate to their students both as individuals *and* as members of the school community at the same time. All members of the community exist in relationship to one another in different kinds of intersecting and overlapping loyalties. Pastoral counselors form an interesting instance of those who sometimes work under the auspices of a church but whose practices are separate from it. Their professional ethics may combine aspects of the different communities to which they are allied.[28]

The implications for confidentiality are significant. It is the inescapable presence of community that presses us to reexamine the notion of confidentiality in the ministry. For one thing, if church people relate to one another both individually and collectively at the same time, then dilemmas about what to say when cannot always be characterized by a clash between the principles of fidelity and justice. Fidelity can no longer signify faithfulness only to individuals and justice can no longer be owed only to groups. A youth group that adopts the covenant "What happens in youth group stays in youth group," is reflecting a sense of fidelity to the *group*. If one member of the group were to decide to break confidentiality in order to seek help for another member, his dilemma would be characterized as one of fidelity to that member versus fidelity to the group. Similarly, the principle of justice does not always correspond to relationships to the wider community. Sometimes one becomes committed to keeping a confidence out of a duty of justice for an individual. A chaplain, for example, who learns that one of his students is gay keeps this information from socially conservative faculty members if he knows that the student would suffer unjustifiably from being "outed" to them. As helpful as the principles of professional ethics often are to help us examine confidentiality, therefore, they do not provide the only way.

Most importantly, the community context of ministry changes ministry ethics by reminding clergy and laypeople that they are never ultimately alone. The building of relationships is always a priority. The implication for confidentiality is not necessarily that all information should be indiscriminately broadcast to the entire community—there is still such a thing as a private realm, as we will see later in this chapter—but that opportunities should always be sought for them to build relationships by entrusting others in the community with the things that matter.

In summary, if we wish to move beyond the simple assertion that ministers should keep silent about everything they hear, it will help to use something besides the ethical frameworks drawn from secular professions, for these frameworks do not always fit the unique character of faith communities. I have argued that relationships within faith communities are ones of trust and that trust relationships grow if they are practiced smartly. Let us turn, therefore, to the features of trust relationship that we have identified and see how they shed light on confidentiality in the ministry. We will consider risk, vulnerability, and power from both the perspective of the confider and the confidant, remembering that these can be groups of people as well as individuals.

RISK, VULNERABILITY, AND POWER: TWO PERSPECTIVES

The Confider's Perspective

Confidentiality will only grow trust between people if both the confider and confidant respect the risk, vulnerability, and power of their relationship. Disclosing something important to another person is often an act of risk. Not everyone is a good confidant, which makes disclosure something of a gamble. It is like handing over something of value. On the one hand, we want our confidants to respond with sensitivity to the information we are sharing, respecting its meaning and importance to us and understanding how we feel. We hope and expect that they will grasp the emotional content of the information, even share our emotion. We also want them to help us out, to play a role, if only by listening, in our transformation from secret keeper to confider. In short, by entrusting them with our secret we ask them to be engaged with us. On the other hand, we expect confidants to be "rocks" for us. We hope they will identify with our emotions but not respond too emotionally themselves. We seek their engagement but hope they will not get overly absorbed in our problem because it remains, after all, still our problem. Above all, when we disclose information to one person or group but request that no one else know, we are asking our confidant(s) to have the knowledge but act as if they do not, at the same time. We give it to them for safekeeping, but not necessarily for use.

Thus, telling a confidence, especially a confession, is a delicate act of establishing trust. It carries all the risks associated with turning over Valued Thing C discussed in chapter 1. The secret is now theirs as well as ours, to do with what they may. As with any trust relationship, we can make an error in judging our risk. Sissela Bok wrote: "One cannot trust all who listen to confessions to be either discreet or especially capable of bringing solace or help."[29] As she points out, the act of confessing can sometimes increase one's risk. Bringing our sins into the light is supposed to be good for us, but in the ears of an incapable confidant, it might not be. Have we not all at one time or another experienced the dismay of confiding in someone and then feeling worse rather than better? If we are not directed toward healing and transformation, our confidence may in retrospect become a risk we should not have taken.

In confiding, especially confessing, a person thus accepts the risk of vulnerability to the other's possible harm. Bonhoeffer knew the vulnerability that the confessing of sins created. While he valued confession as the essential "break-through to fellowship," he recognized its cost. Arguing that in confession we also break through to fellowship with Jesus Christ by accepting our cross, he wrote: "Confession in the presence of a brother is the profoundest kind of humiliation. It hurts, it cuts a man down, it is a dreadful blow to pride. . . . In the confession of sins the old man dies a painful, shameful death before the eyes of a brother."[30] Letting someone else see our sin is a form of vulnerability.

When we confess to another person or community, moreover, we open ourselves to further vulnerability of being probed for yet more information. The initial act of confiding is not the end of the trust relationship. Most of us know that it is possible for confidants to become overly invasive, even when they do not mean to be, once they possess some information. The "therapeutic model" discussed above is likely to promote the belief that secrecy is inherently bad ("pathogenic," as Bok puts it) and self-revelation always a good.[31] Driven by this belief, confidants may press for disclosure beyond the appropriate point, failing to discriminate between what will promote healing and what is merely disclosure for disclosure's sake. At their worst, confidants can manipulate and even coerce confiders. Like the Vicomte de Valmont in *Liaisons Dangereuses*, they may elicit confidences by pretending to reveal their own. They may extend the seductive promise of intimacy, claiming that mutual confession will strengthen their relationship.

Another risk worth mentioning here is the risk that the confidant might *not* breach confidentiality when it would be the best thing for the confider. Sometimes the help people most need is secured only when their secret is shared, and in the best trust relationships Persons A and B leave themselves open to this possibility. One of the cases that first made news as a case of "clergy malpractice" involved a pastor who would not turn outside his counseling relationship for help for a suicidal parishioner. The case was *Nally v. Grace Community Church of the Valley* in California during the 1980s. Kenneth Nally, a member of the church, was in counseling with church pastors when he attempted suicide and was hospitalized. Doctors recommended that he receive professional care from a psychiatrist, but pastor John MacArthur apparently discouraged Nally from seeking it and encouraged him instead to continue in pastoral counseling, to pray, read scripture, and listen to tapes of his (MacArthur's) sermons. Nally committed suicide while staying in MacArthur's home. Nally's father brought a lawsuit against the pastors and the church, alleging that they failed in their duty to provide care for his son and that they knew about his suicidal intentions but failed to refer him to medical professionals. The California Supreme Court eventually found that the defendants could not be held legally accountable for Nally's death, and that imposing a duty of care would "have a deleterious effect on counseling in general," but the lower Court of Appeal had found that the church and its counselors had acted negligently.[32] At issue in this case was whether the First Amendment protected clergy from accountability for harm to a parishioner. Legal issues aside, it also raised serious ethical questions about the limits of keeping information confidential that might rightly be shared in order to provide necessary help to the confider.

As we said earlier, cases like these are extreme and thankfully do not happen often. The point is that a confider thus runs many potential risks and opens herself to unforeseen vulnerabilities. She must heed the rules of trust that we have discussed: even in relationship with a minister, no confider should open herself to so much risk as to do harm to her self. It is very important that the confider be able to choose the risks she takes. In a morally sound trust relationship, Person A should always be in a position to accept the vulnerability to which she exposes herself. As Bok puts it with regard to confession, "So long as the speaker has the freedom to decide how much to reveal and when, and the discretion to exercise this freedom, he will be able to pursue the joint exploration without fear of the risks . . ."[33] Risks will always remain in confiding to others because the future remains open, but confiders can try to take appropriate risks.

Accepting one's own vulnerability requires, of course, that it first be acknowledged. People in church may have to reinstitute their trust relationships before they learn to confide deeply in one another and not simply rest on the assumption that everybody in church is trustworthy because "we've known them forever." The rule of transparency becomes important here as well. A confider can acknowledge her vulnerability before others, not just to herself. After all, most people will want to be trustworthy to someone who says, "This is painful for me to admit, but . . ."

In the confider-confidant relationship as we have been describing it, the confidant has more power. Particularly with ministers and other professionals, the confidant is not expected to share confidences in return. To put it simply, clergy confidentiality represents a unilateral relationship, not a mutual one. This alone gives clergy power over those who tell them their secrets. They also have the power granted to them by virtue of being someone to whom others turn in times of vulnerability. A layperson coming to a clergyperson with a guilty secret is an example of someone whose vulnerability predates the trust relationship and whose power is imbalanced from the start.

In one sense, however, confiders retain at least a certain kind of power. Even in the case of confession, one who tells a secret is taking steps to confront and control their past. Confessing is a way to hold oneself accountable for one's past actions and thus claim responsibility and agency for future ones. The concept of penance, after all, is that one can do something about the past and get started on the future with a clean slate. "Coming forward" by bringing the secret to another person is therefore already in itself a demonstration of power. It should provide to the person who receives the secret some assurance that a change is sought, that the trust relationship will be dynamic rather than static, and that in entrusting the confidant with this symbol of the past and hope for the future, the confider can be trusted in return not to abuse the relationship.

For it is always possible that confidentiality can be used by the confider against the confidant. Let us now consider risk, vulnerability, and power from the other point of view.

The Confidant's Perspective

Clergy can be made vulnerable by the unreasonable expectations about confidentiality held within the church. As we argued above, laypeople both expect clergy to keep silent and to divulge. Both expectations stem from their perceptions of the role of clergy, so one cannot please everyone. On occasion, people in the church will take advantage of unstated assumptions about clergy confidentiality. The ministerial promise of silence has sometimes been called a "shield"—confessions and other confidences are sheltered behind the minister's role. Confiders have been known to invoke the shield after the fact, in order to protect information they come to regret having shared. But if the original context did not warrant a promise of confidentiality, they are unjustified in demanding it later. This is like Person A claiming to Person B that C was valuable and should have been kept safe, when it was not. "But I told you that in confidence!" they cry, hoping to make you feel guilty for having repeated something they said. This in effect becomes reverse coercion, an abuse of the truster's power rather than the entrusted's.

In other ways hearing confidences can become a burden on clergy. If Person A runs a risk in telling their secret to someone who may handle it incompetently, Person B faces the challenge of being a competent and caring listener. It is not always easy to listen well, provide the right kind of solace, and interpret the needs of the confider. In the case of confession, you must provide absolution in a way that asks neither too little nor too much. The burden on the confidant can sometimes genuinely become a risk. The reason Bonhoeffer counseled against one member of the community becoming confessor to all the rest was the danger it presented: "All too easily this one person will be overburdened; thus, confession will become for him an empty routine, and this will give rise to the disastrous misuse of the confessional for the exercise of spiritual domination of souls."[34]

Confidants also run the risk of becoming coercive when they do not intend to be, especially in cases of confession. It may at first glance seem easy to avoid coercing others' confessions. But sometimes people go to great lengths to avoid saying the things they need to say! Denial and self-deception are powerful forces, complicating the process of coming forward with a revelation. When faced with someone who resists or delays telling us what we know they ought to tell, we can become overly zealous in our attempt to work the confidence out of them. The result is a confidence whose voluntariness is forever in doubt. Needless to say, a trust relationship built on such a shaky foundation has limited hope of success. Usually people will find someone else to confide in once they experience us to be at all coercive, and we will have lost our chance to serve as their confidant.

One of the most common risks confidants face is recognizing in time that they are confidants! All too often we realize too late that we are listening to a confidence. Joseph Bush puts it well when he says that confiders frequently "tack in" to their revelations, arriving obliquely rather than directly at the sensitive information they want to share. This makes it difficult to establish the "ground rules" so often advised by those of us who counsel others on this subject. But if confidants could name the vulnerability they experience when caught off guard in this way, confiders might better understand that they cannot unreflectively assume that a promise of silence has been given.

Related to this is the risk of being assumed a confidant when you are not in a position to be one. If you know that in good faith you are supposed to share information you hear with, say, other members of your staff, it is improper to suggest otherwise to those who tell you things. Becoming a confidant, especially early in one's ministry, is rather seductive. One of the "sexy" moments in the ministry (of which there are precious few) is getting to say, "I can't tell you that; it's confidential." Giving into this seduction, however, cuts short the possibility of bringing two other people together for a conversation they need to have. The harder moral action, in other words is declining the privilege of hearing a secret, but this is ultimately what will grow trust within your community.[35]

One might think that one can simply prevent all the situations posed above by always stating up front what the rules of any given confidence will be. In fact, instituting a few rules about confidentiality in the ministry would be a very wise move on the part of clergy. Many problems arise simply because assumptions are not clarified between those who serve and those who are served. The small group ministry cited in chapter 1 should not continue without some mutually understood guidelines, for example, about what kind of information remains inside the circle. But as we know, trust cannot be spelled out in advance or it will cease being trust. Sometimes trust has been known to grow despite, and even because, the entrusted broke a rule. Trust relationships also develop over time, and what seemed initially like an easy confidence to keep can later cry out to be broken. Clergy confidentiality is likely to be one moral problem in the ministry where a combination of contractual and trusting approaches serves best.

PUBLIC AND PRIVATE

Many of the accusations confidants face result from lack of clarity about the nature of the relationship. In the ministry, one often has to discern whether a given relationship is public or private. What is the difference? Public relationships are candid, open, nonexclusive, and often unilateral; they are based on respect and are tied to one's role or function in the community. People in public relationships choose to reveal only what they do not mind everyone knowing and therefore learn to be somewhat guarded. Their actions and positions on public matters are open for debate, and they do not take criticism or praise for them "personally." The point of public relationships is to build community and strive toward shared goals. Public relationships are important, serious, and deeply held, but they do not enter all spheres of life. Private relationships, in contrast, are personal, chosen selectively, closed, based on intimacy and affection, usually mutual, and tied to one's identity, whether familial or personal. People in private relationships share most aspects of their lives with each other. Private relationships provide a safe space for the individual to "be themselves" apart from scrutiny and public attention. They are reserved for the sharing of more intimate and personal information.

The distinction is often a tricky one, especially when it comes to the ministry. Is the small group ministry public or private? An ecumenical Bible study group? The clergy support group a minister belongs to through her denomination? Classes in divinity school? The ministry blogs to which we subscribe? Am I in public or private when I stand in the pulpit? At a bedside? The difficulty answering such questions demonstrates what I believe to be widespread ambivalence and even confusion about the difference between public and private. But the different spheres of relationship require different ethics. If I think we are operating on the basis of a private relationship, then I will tend to assume that what I say stays between us and I will not hear it repeated in public. If, however, I assume we have a public relationship, I will expect both to give and receive information that everyone is free to know. Let us take as an example my views on abortion. In a private relationship I might share my personal history with you, inquire into yours, and tell you that I have agonized over the moral question of whether I would ever seek an abortion if I became pregnant unexpectedly. In a public relationship, on the other hand, I might leave out my personal history and agony and present my convictions with an eye toward articulating a persuasive position. I might appear less personal but equally passionate about the moral issues involved. I would not later claim that I told you my thoughts in confidence.

I am not trying to suggest that the difference between public and private is always crystal clear. In reality they become blurred in many of our relationships. More importantly, neither do I claim to be able to resolve the question of whether relationships in the church are public or private. They probably lie somewhere in the middle, depending on the community. I raise the importance of distinguishing public and private, however, because decisions about confidentiality so often hinge on doing so. In fact, the distinction contributes to the very definitions of confider and confidant. Earlier, we defined confidentiality as the telling of a secret with a promise attached. If there is no promise, then confidentiality cannot necessarily be demanded. But if a promise exists either explicitly or implicitly, it should normally be kept. When people are uncertain about the nature of the relationship, though, they can put the people with whom they speak in a vulnerable position, not knowing whether they will eventually be resented for what they repeat or deemed an untrustworthy confidant. Ambivalence around public and private is one of the things that can make sustaining, sound trust relationships such a difficult undertaking.

ETHICS OF CLERGY CONFIDENTIALITY

We are now in a position to summarize the ethics of clergy confidentiality according to an ethic of trust. We will primarily consider the perspective of the minister who hears confidences. The confider's level of risk must be a factor in whether a minister decides to promise silence or not. Trust relationships are destroyed when the entrusted makes the truster take too great a risk. So, for example, if a parishioner approaches her priest and despite trepidation summons the courage to tell the story of being an incest survivor, or a binge eater, or a mother who sometimes screams at her children, her risk in revealing the story should generally be honored. Her priest may eventually assist her to seek further help by confiding in others who can tell similar stories, but for now their trust relationship is built upon the fact that she went out on a limb. To force her further out would be morally unjustifiable. If, on the other hand, in a coffee-hour conversation with her priest a parishioner confesses to a daily chocolate habit, her priest would be under little obligation, in my view, to guard this secret carefully. (This does not mean the priest should gossip about this, and certainly she is obligated not to use the information in such a way as to embarrass her parishioner.) In most communities that I know of, admitting to a chocolate craving does not represent an undue risk.

Part of the minister's role is to support people in taking as much risk as is appropriate, based on the premise "the greater the risk, the greater the trust." One of the things wrong with following a rule of universal clergy silence is that it makes things too easy. It fails to encourage members of a community to take the risks that allow trust to flourish. This is not an invitation to break promises one has made. It is a call to remind folks that in genuine Christian community all are there to listen. As Willimon says: "Indeed, one of the primary goals of pastoral care ought to be encouraging private pain to 'go public' as soon as possible. That does not mean that I will divulge something a parishioner has said to me in confidence. It does mean that I help the troubled individual to see that the main resource for pastoral care in the church is the whole church."[36]

When it comes to risk, the confidant's risk should be commensurate with the confider's. The more risky it is for one person to tell a secret, the more risky it probably is for the confidant to keep it. The reason is that there are likely third parties not only interested in the information but also affected by not knowing it. Keeping a confidence from these interested parties is tantamount to excluding them. After all, as we said earlier, agreeing to confidentiality is implicating oneself in secrecy, and this usually carries risk. But trust relationships depend on matching risk with risk. Recalling one of the maxims for winning at the Prisoner's Dilemma, we can affirm the moral importance of giving "tit-for-tat" when it comes to confidentiality.

Confidences should not be an occasion to exacerbate anyone's vulnerability or create a power struggle. Part of the reason I have dwelt upon the risks undertaken by confidants as well as confiders is simply to underscore the mutual nature of this trust relationship.

When one person tells a secret to another, or to a group, a trust relationship is immediately implied. Often, however, the issues of risk, vulnerability, and power relevant to the relationship are not immediately obvious. The moral questions often get reduced to justifying the circumstances under which a confider can breach the confidentiality agreement after the fact. I would argue that a sparing use of confidentiality will make confiders and confidants take all the more seriously the relationships they *do* form.

Chapter Three

✺ MISCONDUCT

W ill checking up on church leaders assure us that they are trustworthy? It would seem ministerial misconduct in the church provides the classic example of a time when trusting reliance ought to be combined with healthy distrust. When entrusted people abuse their power, one prudent response is to institute some explicit assurances against future risk, in the form of limitations upon who else may be entrusted and/or checks into past behavior. Indeed, it might seem cruel to talk to a community affected by misconduct about accepting vulnerability to potential harm, as we have defined trust. As I affirmed in chapter 1, a trust relationship is neither the only nor the wisest form of relationship. However, I also affirmed that even when a more formal, contractual form of relationship is sought, trust remains indispensable. In this chapter, then, I hope to show that while ministerial misconduct may present the strongest case for supplementing the practice of trust with other measures, the smart practice of trust should continue to be fostered. I will further show that sometimes formal measures intended to prevent misconduct can not only backfire but also foreclose the possibility of trust.

Accounting theorist Michael Power, author of *The Audit Society*, would say that checking up on people or their work does not necessarily make them more trustworthy.[1] An "audit" may be defined broadly as any kind of check into other people's behavior or practices. An "audit society" is one where formal, third-party verification and certification procedures have overtaken ordinary interpersonal trust relationships, to the extent that people do not necessarily trust each other any more but bestow their trust in these audit mechanisms. A classic example is the criminal background check, which screens individuals by auditing their history with the law. Background checks are becoming increasingly popular in the ministry, because people think that their use will prevent misconduct from happening in the church. Power contends, however, that not only do auditing practices like these fail to accomplish their own presumed goal of reassuring concerned communities, but they also actually jeopardize trust by replacing trust in persons with trust in procedures. I agree, and I believe it is time to question our increasing reliance on background checks and other such "audits."

Of course, scrutinizing ministers' behavior is nothing new. Church leaders have always been subject to certain forms of scrutiny. "Living in the parsonage next to the church" is practically a trope for being subjected to the attentions of parishioners. Of course, clergy complain about this because parishioners sometimes don't know how to allow them any privacy at all. But with the advent of the kinds of procedures Power calls audit, both the scope and type of scrutiny is changing. Communities of faith are turning more and more to formal, detailed, less relational methods of ensuring trustworthy ministry. And they do not stop at ordained professional leaders but include lay leaders as well if they are in positions of responsibility for caring for vulnerable individuals. In other words, the ministry is developing its own "audits" for the same reason other professions have: they are supposed to increase trustworthiness and reduce risk. Concerns over safety drive a community to find objective, measurable tests to ensure compliance with standards for minimizing risk. Audits produce a sense of security, and security is needed in an age where revelations of misconduct are increasingly commonplace.

The name we most commonly give to these sorts of tests and procedures is "safe church practices." Safe church practices are a response, as we know, to mounting revelations of clergy sexual misconduct. Recent disclosures of misconduct have served as an overdue wake-up call for the profession of ministry—and deservedly so, for misconduct is wrong in any profession but particularly egregious when trust is abused by those ordained to stand with others before God. The point here is not to argue against safe church measures, for any misconduct thwarted is a grave harm prevented. The point, rather, is to question whether such measures will work in the long run or whether practicing better, smarter trust would be more successful. Let me repeat this: I am not necessarily advocating against forms of audit in the ministry—I would support several of them—but I am skeptical of the ultimate effectiveness of audit practices alone to deliver the assurance that vulnerable people deserve. As I argued in chapter 1, we need to find some way to entrust ourselves to each other, and sometimes formal systems and structures and rules are the answer to human vulnerability. But interpersonal trust will always be necessary and therefore, despite its difficulty, we cannot live without it. Ultimately, nothing we do can absolutely lock in trustworthiness, and in the rush to audit, we may lose the ability to put our trust in trust.

EVOLUTION OF RESPONSES TO MISCONDUCT

I believe there is reason to worry about the new trend in safe church practices, but let me consider an objection right at the outset: perhaps the ministry has simply been slow to respond to the reality of misconduct and that the time has long passed for us to be instituting the kind of formalities to which professionals in other realms have already acclimated themselves. Maybe the ministers who grumble about having to supply a background check in order to get a job are simply bellyaching, reacting the way other professionals once did who initially opposed the bureaucratization of their practices. Do pastors and priests just have to become accustomed to practicing ministry under new levels of scrutiny the way they have had to get used to nosy parishioners? Do Sunday school teachers simply have to resign themselves to getting fingerprinted? It could be argued that we in the church are merely experiencing an early stage of the inevitable process of calling ourselves to greater account and that in such a stage, any group will tend to miss the way things were in the "old days."

Ethicist Caroline Whitbeck writes about the stages of acceptance and change regarding responsible conduct within a very different community, that of research science. Looking retrospectively at the last several decades of steady effort to improve the integrity of scientific research, she identifies three distinct periods. (Misconduct in a scientific context takes the form, for example, of plagiarism and the falsification of data in order to publish desirable results.) The first period was marked by stubborn silence punctuated by a few solitary warnings. In other words, the research community largely denied that misconduct in their laboratories was any problem at all. Whitbeck says that the prevailing opinion during these early years was that offenses were extremely rare in the profession and perpetrated only by crazy, isolated practitioners. This assumption was, of course, dangerously misleading. Intentionally comparing research misconduct to child sexual abuse, Whitbeck writes about how dangerous a mind-set of denial can be: "Most investigators would not commit research misconduct any more than most adults would molest children, yet the perpetrators of both sorts cannot be easily picked out and misconduct happens frequently enough to require better measures of control."[2]

The second period began when the government stepped in to mandate procedures for handling misconduct after some egregious cases were bungled. This led to grudging recognition on the part of researchers of the need for research conduct guidelines. At the same time, however, it also led to polarized debate about how best to institute them. The rhetoric degenerated largely into one of legalism, as scientists argued over what precisely constituted falsification and fraud, and over just how misconduct ought to be defined.

Whitbeck is confident that the scientific research community has moved into a third period, this one marked by the emergence of more reasoned discourse and more nuanced consideration of what promotes responsible conduct. Institutions accept the need not only to be regulated, she says, but also to take active steps toward inculcating a culture of responsibility. For example, instructors now even recognize that they must teach research integrity to their students. (We in the ministry call this process "formation.") Only now in this third phase has the research community begun to employ a rhetoric of ethics and trust, and to make room for what Whitbeck terms "subtler issues of responsibility and trustworthiness."[3]

Some churches, as well as some individual church members of most churches, undoubtedly find themselves today in Whitbeck's "stage one." They continue to deny even the possibility of ministerial misconduct. I still hear people say things like, "I just can't believe that any minister would hurt a child. They're *ministers*." These people want to rest in the state of naïve trust. Other churches find themselves in the second stage. They acknowledge the possibility of ministerial misconduct, they have perhaps heard about cases in neighboring towns, and they accept the fact that they ought to put some safe church policies in place. The companies that insure them insist on such policies, furthermore, so they do what they have to do to keep their insurance. Finally, some communities undoubtedly represent the final stage; they have not only enacted policies and procedures but have also educated themselves and worked to instill a culture of integrity in ministerial relationships and intolerance to misconduct.

What worries me, however, is the possibility that Whitbeck's narrative of denial, regulation, and cultural transformation may not always be so linear. Do communities always move progressively from one to the other? Is it not possible that acquiescence to regulation may represent a step backward? It does not seem to me that communities always emerge from internal bickering ready to engage in subtler discourses about trust. Rather, their bickering is too often quieted in a collective sigh: acquiescence to externally defined procedures for risk management. (In the science community, it was largely the federal government that stepped in to provide regulation, because it is a significant funder of research. In the church, insurance companies appear to be playing this role.) This does not necessarily represent awareness of the need for trust. Therefore, I am concerned that many churches will simply stay content to abide by safe church rules that have largely been pressed upon them from outside.

Another way to look at the proliferation of safe church practices is to see them as the latest attempt to seek reassurance regarding ministerial conduct, replacing previous attempts that did not fully succeed. Historically, ministers like other professionals were considered trustworthy because they were counted on to regulate themselves. Self-regulation has even been considered by many a hallmark of what it means to be a professional. Professional practice—as in medicine and law and the ministry—has traditionally been organized around internal standards for acceptable and unacceptable practice; laypeople have been expected to accept and trust these standards. Another way of putting it is that every profession has always had its quacks, and, correspondingly, ways of identifying and stigmatizing quackery. But this has been done entirely by those inside the guild. Legitimate practitioners were counted on to expose the sellers of snake oil and oust them from their profession. Professionals, in other words, have traditionally held themselves accountable and by themselves reassured their trusting laity against concerns about risk.

But entrusting a group to regulate itself is always problematic. It simply has its limits. It is like a "blind," uninformed trust relationship existing within an imbalance of power. Historically, therefore, nearly all professions at some point came under additional accountability to some form of outside legislation, be it state or federal law or the policies of some regulatory agency. Today most professionals are expected to meet both internal and external standards of accountability. Laypeople and practitioners have recourse to both if they suspect wrongdoing. This reduces their vulnerability. In addition, many professions have come over time to adopt some sort of contractual system between client and professional, enforceable by law. In medicine, for example, consent forms and living wills were introduced to reduce risk. A form of contract, they make explicit doctors' responsibilities toward their patients and give patients a means of redress if the responsibilities are disregarded. In the terms we used in chapter 1, a feeling of trust can sometimes be secured through contract.

Interestingly, however, even these measures have proven insufficient within an increasing number of professions. Recent history has seen the introduction of newer, additional attempts to secure professional trustworthiness. These are the various forms of verification and monitoring and checking up that we are calling "audit." Audit has not replaced contract, but it is increasingly popular as an additional form of control and assurance. Audits add a layer of detail (and bureaucracy) that is new. An example of audit from the realm of academia is the emergent phenomenon of outcome assessment. It is no longer sufficient that a teacher produce a syllabus in order to hold herself accountable to her students; she must now additionally demonstrate at the end of the course that she taught what she said she would teach. Schools now not only grant degrees as proof of students' learning and achievement, but now also issue formal assessment results (to accrediting bodies and parents and the students themselves). Audits represent the next step communities are taking to reassure themselves in the wake of misconduct. The question is whether they will work any better. Though she does not use the term *audit*, British philosopher Onora O'Neill observes the shift I am talking about:

> In the last twenty years in many parts of the world further measures have been introduced, which introduce more precise ways of securing better and more detailed compliance with externally imposed requirements, and so (it is supposed) increased trustworthiness. . . . It is an agenda of replacing traditional relations of trust, now grown problematic, with stronger systems for securing trustworthiness.[4]

O'Neill is one of the foremost philosophers of trust today, and she is doubtful that these "stronger systems" will actually strengthen trust. Finally, for me, the question is this: Were traditional relations of trust problematic and therefore genuinely in need of replacement, or were they poorly practiced and in need of repair?

SAFE CHURCH PRACTICES

Let us examine some of the measures for preventing and responding to ministerial misconduct that are being introduced in churches today, for they most closely correspond to audits. We will look in turn at the screens used in recruiting staff, checklists for the church's physical environment, requirements for leadership of ministry programs, and rules governing clergy behavior. After we begin in this section to analyze and critique safe church practices, we will in the next section compare them to audits.

Churches concerned about misconduct, first of all, seek to be assured about the quality of their leaders, both paid and volunteer. Anyone who ministers in the church's name can come into intimate contact with individuals, so we must all be able to rely on them to serve responsibly. To feel confident in their reliance, and to help ensure that those who work for the church will not hurt others in their care, churches have taken to screening workers before they start work. Screening measures currently being introduced include written applications, interviews, reference checks, home visits, observations, psychological evaluation, fingerprinting, and criminal background checks. When deciding which screens to employ for which workers, church leaders often match the level of scrutiny and intensity necessary to the level of responsibility a worker will have. For example, those who will minister directly and regularly with large numbers of children and youth, and those who might spend time alone and away from church with young people, are checked out more comprehensively than the occasional Sunday school substitute or youth group chaperone. More information is verified about candidates of the former type by casting the net wider for potentially incriminating information about them. One manual, suggesting three levels of screening, explained this rule of thumb:

> The kinds of information collected at each level of screening are basically the same. But the source of screening information is different. At the basic level, the primary source of the information is the applicant or references selected by the applicant. At the intermediate level, the sources of information expand to include: state and local criminal history records; references who supervised the applicant in similar positions, both paid and volunteer; and, personal observation and home visitations. For comprehensive screening, the possible sources expand to include national record checks, specialized state and local registries and data bases; and intensive interviewing and testing.[5]

On the surface, the implementation of screening procedures for church workers seems unarguably sensible. Clearly, it is a desirable goal to uncover any troubling information about an individual before she or he begins serving in the church. This goal is promoted not only by church insurance agencies and ecclesiastical bodies whose responsibility it is to respond to and adjudicate misconduct after it happens, but also by people in the church who are committed to reducing the risk of harm beforehand, especially on behalf of the most vulnerable among them.

Upon closer consideration, however, screening procedures may not achieve their desired goal. Why? The primary reason is that screens contain an inherent Catch-22: make them too effective and you lose too many people. Think of a literal screen. If it is woven loosely it lets a lot of air and sunshine through, but also particles of dust and debris. If woven too finely, it traps most of the undesirable particles but also becomes too opaque to see through. The analogy to workplace screening procedures should be obvious. A rudimentary search to reveal that a particular volunteer's references check out, and that he has committed no felonies in the state, cannot assure us that he will never harm a child. Unless all we care about is holding back the rare individual who has been discovered, arrested, and convicted of a violent crime, our search will be less than fully effective in safeguarding us against future risk. There are, unfortunately, many more individuals beyond this rare individual who have the potential to become dangerous. As we have all learned from the tragic school shooting incidents that make national news, a troubled individual can pass the background checks required to purchase a gun and still end up killing several people. On a different level, we probably all know of professionals who passed the entrance exams required by their guild and still committed misconduct.

On the other hand, a thoroughgoing search to identify all the possible red flags raised by someone's personality or character would be so oner-ous as to prove unworkable in most churches. Few of us, I suspect, would want to put ordinary church workers through the kind of psychological interviewing, testing, or home visitation that might eventually prove them unsuitable in some way for working in the church. (We might be willing to take some if not all of these measures when certifying candidates for ordination.) Such a screen becomes too "costly" to employ. And yet it is really the only way to identify and therefore hold back the people who have a predilection for misconduct. In short, screens that are designed to sift through candidates thoroughly enough to provide reassurance may end up working so well that they defeat their own purpose: they will tend to be abandoned. It is in the nature of screens, therefore, to be difficult to design one that is neither too loose nor too tight but to get one that will actually yield the right candidates and provide genuine security. *This* is why they are less effective in preventing misconduct than they initially appear.

A second reason screens may not achieve their desired goal is a psychological one. Especially when implemented in the absence of other approaches to risk reduction, screening procedures tend to be met with resistance. It seems to be endemic to human nature that the innocent and guilty alike balk at investigative scrutiny. A check into our background, designed as it is to ferret out potentially negative information, cannot help but feel to us like suspicion, no matter how much we tell ourselves that we are not actually being suspected of wrongdoing and that the procedure is serving ultimately to keep us safe. (How many of us, after all, express our gratitude to the airport personnel who subject us and our belongings to detection?)

Checks like these are not designed, after all, to uncover our positive qualities. The function of a "screen" is to hold back any undesirable entities and passively let the good ones fall through. In the absence of efforts by those doing the recruiting to uncover our good attributes (like our strengths and qualifications for a job), even a voluntary consent to have our record checked tends to feel burdensome and invite resentment. People's resistance may therefore over time undermine the overall goal of reducing risk in the church because qualified potential volunteers will simply turn away. One manual puts it this way: "The volunteer force for the nursery could grow precariously slim because congregational members resist going through a screening process. . . . At this point, church leaders may be tempted to abandon, ignore, or severely curtail the risk reduction program."[6]

The process of screening church workers could contain a third, related danger. It might suggest to some people a suspicious attitude on the part of the church toward those who might want to become more involved in its ministries. Listing some of the reasons why the church has been slow to respond to the crisis of sexual abuse, one text reads: "We want to think the best of people and to welcome people into our midst. We believe that those who attend church with us will be striving to live Christian lives. We feel that 'screening' may give the message that a person is 'welcome,' but with certain conditions."[7] While the author meant this to be an example of a false ideology standing in the way of change, there is a grain of truth to it. If within a particular congregation, the practice of getting to know people better is limited to the applications and interviews they must undergo in order to volunteer, it might be justifiably argued that the church's welcome is less than robust! If all newcomers were regularly visited, introduced, and welcomed into the various ministries of the church, quite apart from volunteer screening procedures, then an interview to become a church school teacher would not be associated with an attempt to keep some folks away. A community that genuinely and consistently practiced hospitality to the stranger—not to mention longtime members—could institute extra procedures for checking up on potential volunteers without giving the impression of suspicion. Getting to know one another would be woven into the fabric of congregational life and would not seem like an "extra" effort at all. Too often, however, churches neglect precisely this kind of ongoing relationship building.

Similarly, churches that only pay attention to people's qualifications for leadership when they step forward to volunteer send a message that they only hope their people meet minimal standards of competency. Churches that instead institute regular, sustainable training for people in leadership positions convey the sense that they care about the quality of leadership in their church. If we only engage people when the time to enlist new volunteers rolls around, this has a dampening effect on both people's enthusiasm for their work and the quality of the work itself.[8]

Finally, since many screening procedures, like criminal record checks and psychological evaluations, involve parties external to the church, churches run the risk of imposing an impersonal and unfamiliar authority upon the community. Depending on the tradition to which the church belongs and, moreover, its historical and theological attitudes toward secular authority instituting a system of checks like these may generate complaints about "meddling" that are difficult to placate. Polities that have historically viewed the church as standing over and against the world do not adapt easily to the institution of worldly approval ratings.

All this is not to say that volunteer screening programs should not be implemented. But in the end, their value is mostly limited to what we will in a moment call "negative assurance." All they can do is tell us what is not there. This limited value must be borne in mind lest overconfidence be built up. "Even the most extensive volunteer screening process has limitations. Organizations should be cautious not to succumb to a false sense of security. Organizational leaders need other preventive strategies to supplement volunteer screening, once it is up and running."[9] In fact, screening procedures may ultimately backfire; that is, they may actually contribute to the difficulties of relying on others and reducing risk. Thus, the best ones do not exist in isolation but represent only one part of a comprehensive approach to preventing misconduct.

The church's physical environment is another area of concern because misconduct usually happens in contexts of isolation. Reconfiguring layout and space is therefore a second kind of safe church practice. It is increasingly common, for instance, to see churches redesigning the floor plan of their educational spaces so as to create large open rooms rather than multiple separate rooms where interactions between adults and children might be obscured. Bathrooms are being relocated near the classrooms for the younger ages so that children can be monitored but not necessarily accompanied. Other strategies in this category include locating clergy offices in an area of the church that sees the most traffic so that the ministers remain as much as possible in plain view. Staff members who counsel individuals in the church may be required to keep their doors open. "A window in every door removes the opportunity for secrecy and isolation, conditions every abuser seeks."[10] The goal here, of course, is to minimize any temptation on the part of volunteers and staff to take advantage of isolation by making their activities visible and accountable to all. This is a laudable goal and probably works. The goal for the rest of the community, in addition to sending the message that they will not tolerate misconduct, is essentially to provide the possibility of "spot checking" staff behavior. One way of describing open space is to see it as an opportunity for the wider community to view at any time a representative "sample" of the work going on so as to verify its trustworthiness. This goal, in contrast, may be less achievable than we think, as we shall see in a moment.

Unfortunately, abusers intent on causing harm can find their way around design changes to create the conditions they seek. A window in every door may furthermore remove the opportunity for privacy sought by individuals seeking help. Some people may hesitate to approach the ministerial staff if they know that their meeting will be, in effect, public. Once again, a strategy for verifying the trustworthiness of a ministry professional can ironically undermine an actual attempt at building trust. The church must find a way to improve the safety of its environment while not giving up too much in the way of values like privacy. We said in chapter 1 that trust was like moving ahead while accepting potential but unanticipated harm. Likewise, to become a safe church, we must try to imagine the unimaginable—the possibility that someone within the community might betray us—and at the same time, move forward by ensuring that the remedy is not worse than the risk. This balancing act is no easy task but it is crucial both to the safety of the powerless and to the survival of the trusting community that is the church.

A third strategy for risk reduction is adopting a set of rules about who can minister to whom in the church and the conditions under which that ministry will be take place. Rules are especially relevant to programs with children and youth where the need to prevent sexual abuse is considered even greater. Congregations have become increasingly aware of the danger inherent in entrusting the care of children and youth to just anyone. Some examples of new program requirements include the "five-years-older" rule (mandating that volunteers be at least five years older than the people they serve, especially pertinent to youth ministry); a minimum volunteer age of eighteen (prohibiting younger teens from accepting responsibility for children); the "two-adult" rule (requiring that any children's program be staffed by two adults so that none is ever left alone with children); parental notice (asking parents to give permission for their children's participation in programs away from church); covenants (having volunteers sign written statements every year, outlining the values and practices to be followed in the program); mandatory annual orientations and training sessions; and measures aimed at health and safety such as training in CPR, first aid, and discipline policies.[11]

These rules are difficult to criticize because they make sense on other grounds besides risk reduction. It is always better to involve more, rather than fewer, adults in the church's educational ministries. Children and adults both benefit from intergenerational interaction. And trained, conscientious volunteers are certainly preferable to untrained ones! The point to be made here is simply that such rules should be introduced carefully so that the community will embrace them as good practice, not simply as a bunch of new rules that now have to be kept. Since many of these rules are difficult to institute in smaller congregations, they can initially seem like impossible mandates and leave people feeling frustrated rather than safe. Indeed, safe church experts say that to be successful, policies designed to guard against misconduct must be instituted by the community as part of an overall campaign for change, and this usually depends on education about the need for risk reduction and the meaning of a safe church. One training manual warns:

> Most churches must undergo substantial organizational change to successfully initiate and sustain a child sexual abuse risk reduction program. . . .

Changing the church is not easy. Like any other complex organization, a church will tend to resist change and maintain the status quo. Yet attempting to force change without the understanding and support of church members and workers can generate negative reactions. The education and training of church members can alleviate much of the distress involved in change.[12]

This manual goes on to suggest that church leaders should assess their church's readiness for change in its programs by looking at how the community has handled transition in the past, how much clarity members tend to expect in new policies and procedures, what sources of authority are most respected when it comes to instituting change, and how congruent the changes are with the church's mission. Change assessments like these are crucial to the establishment and maintenance of trust within organizations like the church. Top-down strategies for promoting (or salvaging) trust tend not to work—except in those organizations that traditionally respond to top-down authority. Thus, community leaders are wise to look to the ways trust has been practiced in the past.

Of course, a different danger associated with introducing change is not that it will be too difficult but that it will go down too easily! The seeming simplicity and reasonableness of safe church practices may itself be the very thing that thwarts their effectiveness. It might be all too easy for a congregation to agree to the kinds of risk reduction strategies just listed, and ignore all the cultural changes that go into becoming a community that is genuinely safe from misconduct. Sexual misconduct, in particular, is fueled by deeply rooted attitudes about gender, authority, and power, and will only finally be prevented when those attitudes are challenged and overhauled. This is far from simple work. In other words, safety rules and procedures are like background checks: they can lull a congregation into thinking it has done "enough."

A fourth type of misconduct prevention, in addition to screening procedures, architectural changes, and program requirements, concerns itself with rules or guidelines for ministerial conduct. Drawing upon what they have learned about the conditions that have bred misconduct, churches are attempting to minimize those conditions. Conduct guidelines are most often implemented for ordained clergy. They include some of the rules already mentioned, such as never counseling parishioners in isolation, but also include reducing or eliminating such practices as home visits, socializing with parishioners, hugging and kissing, and especially dating parishioners. The point is to prevent the practice or even the appearance of sexualized relationships between clergy and the laypeople under their care. The ultimate aim is to circumscribe a boundary within the ministry around intimate, sexual behavior in order to preserve ministers' real work. A Lutheran publication put it this way:

> The pastoral relationship proceeds with the aim of connecting the parishioner to the Gospel in a lifegiving, saving, healing and renewing way. . . . The boundary in the pastor/parishioner relationship is a limit in the kinds of activity that can take place within or around that relationship, limits that provide for a safe connection, bringing the parishioner and the Gospel together.[13]

At the same time, it is important to avoid the appearance that the church is placing arbitrary restrictions on the pastor/parishioner relationship. In the ministry, relationships form the content of the work. To neglect or undermine them is to do a bad job as a minister. Thus, the danger of putting arbitrary or unreasonable restrictions on conduct is the possibility that they might thwart the very work the minister is called to perform. If the steps implemented to ensure parishioners' trust in their pastor seem to stray too far from the point, or even impede the relationship, moreover, parishioners will recoil. Such restrictions may also undermine the building of trust relationships by training people's attention on the rules instead of each other. To use the analogy of driving in traffic, it would be like obeying all the traffic signals and signs but failing to keep an eye out on the other drivers. The same publication therefore urges churches not to dwell too long on this kind of safe church practice. Putting it simply: "Skip the laundry list of don'ts."

> Rigid "laundry lists" of forbidden acts—for example, no touching, no hugging, no closed doors, no home visits—all have the effect of creating a climate of fear, anxiety and mistrust in the congregation. A negative mentality builds up as everyone becomes preoccupied with what can't be done. A stubborn, obstinate spirit develops, as laity and clergy both determine to "break those dumb rules." Rules replace relationships as a focus of concern.[14]

"Skipping the laundry list of don'ts" does not leave congregations with nothing to do. After all, there is plenty to be done in the way of focusing concern on relationships rather than rules. In addition, congregations can work to establish a "zero tolerance" culture, whereby everyone understands that they can freely refuse unwanted conduct without fear of recrimination. Such a practice leaves room for flexibility around certain conduct such as the occasional hug because it empowers each person to define the parameters of tolerable behavior. It encourages the practice of discernment on the part of clergy and laity alike, rather than reliance on rules that might just beg to be broken. Empowering everyone and teaching them to practice wise discernment is a more challenging undertaking, perhaps, than obedience to rules, but it is central to the ongoing practice of trust and a more hopeful path to change in the long run.

Closely related to clergy conduct guidelines, finally, are parameters related to what is commonly called "clergy self-care." Since the evidence suggests that clergy are tempted to engage in misconduct when they are overworked, frustrated, and tired, churches now recognize that encouraging their clergy to take better care of themselves is one way to prevent misconduct. Congregations can insist that their clergy observe regular days off, take their maximum vacation time, and utilize services for mental and spiritual health. They can support clergy in practices like regular exercise and moderate drinking and eating. Like any of the measures previously discussed, self-care measures are sensible and valuable. But their relationship to misconduct prevention is indirect at best. Abuse does not result directly from overwork (although it can be a factor). Abuse has many other indicators that may be far more subtle and difficult to detect. Thus, self-care habits can still mask a troubled personality. Moreover, too often self-care measures are presented in the form of standardized checklists that are inevitably rudimentary. A good score on a self-care checklist is like a clean background check: it does not in itself guarantee a trustworthy leader.[15]

COMPARING SAFE CHURCH PRACTICES AND AUDITS

In describing some of the current trends toward making our churches safer from misconduct, and our leaders more trustworthy, I have already indicated what I believe to be some of the pitfalls of these attempts. They often contain dangers that are not easily seen at first. I will be the first to acknowledge, however, that safe church practices are not going to go away any time soon. If anything, they will probably increase in popularity and intensity. I say this not simply because insurance companies mandate them. Even more significant is that while procedures and rules and screens may meet with resistance, ultimately people believe in them. At some level deeper than their initial distaste, people have faith in their efficacy. Even in the church, we are becoming a society that puts its trust in standards and their compliance.

As I indicated in the introduction to this chapter, a societal shift toward reliance on verification and monitoring has been observed by others whose area of interest lies outside the ministry. Let us compare the trend toward safe church practices with similar trends in other realms, so as to try to understand both why such practices are popular and also why they fail despite their popularity.

The irony lying at the heart of the use of audits, according to Michael Power, is that they often fail to meet the expectations they raise, and yet people's confidence in them does not seem to wane. We should be clear that we are not simply talking about actual auditing procedures but also about the very idea of audit. (This is why we can extrapolate from the world of accounting to the world of ministry.) Auditing refers to one way that organizations and communities attempt to solve the problem of risk reduction. According to the classic meaning of the term, it is a procedure whereby an organization calls upon an independent investigator who in turn asks the organization for an accounting of its practice. The accounting is rendered in the form of selected sample pieces of evidence of that practice. These samples are then examined and interpreted by the auditor whose job it is to certify the practice as sound (or not). The definition of an audit thus includes certain important features: an investigator who is a third party to the practice, the use of and reliance upon select tangible evidence, and a clearly detailed final assessment that can be disseminated to interested parties. Let us consider these features in turn.

The very need for an audit arises in the first place because people in an organization (in accounting theory they are usually called "principals") do not know enough about what is going on to monitor it themselves and be assured that a good job is being done. They may be clients of the organization, students, patients, stockholders—or parishioners. They know they must rely on the leaders within their organization (usually called "practitioners") who are performing work on their behalf. But they cannot rest entirely sure in their reliance, either because they cannot always be present, or because they are not expert enough to judge the work. This asymmetry of knowledge between principal and practitioner prompts the principal to turn to an independent, outside expert who is supposedly in a position to know more about what the practitioner has been up to. This is like parishioners turning to a legal authority to check into a person's background, or like ordination committees turning to a psychologist to certify a candidate's mental health. But experts' independence is both an advantage and a disadvantage. They are by definition outsiders and therefore do not know how the practice is carried out in that particular organization. They do not know the work from the inside, if you will, despite being experts in the practice. Therefore, while they can help compensate for the asymmetry of knowledge, they can never close the trust gap between principals and practitioners. The auditor can never know enough about what corners might be getting cut—or, conversely, what unorthodoxies might actually be legitimate—to provide the principal with total assurance. The insurance company, for example, might issue a mandate to carve a window into the pastor's door but fail to take into account the fact that most of her parishioners commute to and from their jobs, so she tends to meet them after work—the same time her assistant is away. Unless the auditors become so a part of the organization as to make the audit impractical, they cannot give a full and accurate picture of the practice as it is being carried out in that particular context. Therefore, when principals are forced to turn to an outsider to assure themselves of good practice, it is in one sense already too late. No third party can mend the rift such a move represents.

Another part of the problem is selective sampling, which brings us to audit's reliance on evidence. As we have seen from our discussion of trust, if Person A had enough evidence to confirm Person B's trustworthiness, there would be no need to investigate further. When principals ask for an audit, it is because the evidence available to them (of, say, a person's fitness to be a youth group leader or the child care practices used in the nursery) is somehow inconclusive. Therefore, it needs to be tested. But how many pieces of it are sufficient for the auditor to test? How deeply should the auditor look into the practitioner's past and present activities? (How much background checking is enough? How many surprise visits to the nursery should parents make?) In the history of the development of auditing practice, auditors themselves found that they could not possibly check every single transaction. So they decided to take samples and count on these to represent the whole. If the samples were free of error, so, presumably, would be the whole practice.

Obviously there is room for significant cracks through which bad practice can slip. Samples might not represent the whole at all. But one simply cannot afford to "overaudit." Therefore, in practice, the number of samples taken in an audit is balanced against the cost or efficiency of conducting it. Another way of putting it is that in the process of making a practice auditable, complexity has to be ignored. Therefore, Power writes, "Images of control over pollution and derivatives, of higher quality teaching, of improved financial management [of safer churches], and so on get manufactured by an audit process which necessarily insulates itself from organizational complexity in order to make things auditable and to produce certificates of comfort."[16]

Auditors eventually figured out that they did not necessarily even need to check sample transactions at all. Rather, they could leave that task to the organization and instead check up on the organization's practices of monitoring its own transactions. The organization would monitor itself by way of internal controls. This would certainly be more efficient. But relying on internal controls turns auditing into a second-order phenomenon: an audit becomes a process of checking up on the process of checking up. As Power puts it, eventually "the system [rather than the work itself] becomes the primary auditable object."[17] This creates further distance and cracks, however, that mistakes can fall through. It leaves room for the possibility that the organization could present a viable system of controls and its practitioners still be operating poorly or even fraudulently. So long as insiders can decide what is relevant and worth checking, outsiders are effectively marginalized and thus unable to catch the real problems. Ultimately, the whole point of calling for an outside inspection is thrown into question.

Audits are also used to check up on the final product of a given operation. Quality control is a very popular use of audit these days. It pervades many practices and professions, from environmental protection to psychotherapy to academia. The driving force seems, again, to be the desire on the part of principals to make up for their inability to assess practice. But since it is manifestly difficult in most professions to measure or even define quality, it being so subjective a feature of practice, when quality must be proven, systems must be developed to demonstrate it. Practitioners must figure out a set of indicators that will demonstrate to auditors the consistent and verifiable quality of their work. Whether this ultimately improves quality or simply controls the level of quality that already exists is unclear. Actual quality can remain elusive and audits may simply mask poor performance. Power describes the logic with more than a hint of sarcasm: "without audit and the certification that follows from audit, quality remains too private an affair. One might conclude that there is no quality without quality assessment."[18]

Nevertheless, those who have asked for the audit in the first place still hope to be reassured by the auditor's eventual findings. While they may have asked for the audit because they had some worries or concerns, their foremost desire is to be shown a report that proves no wrongdoing. Principals may hope to ferret out instances of misconduct if any exist (the way parishioners may hope to weed out any criminals who want to volunteer in the church) but their preference is to confirm their initial trust in what is going on. In the auditing world, this is termed "negative assurance." We want to be assured that something is not present or has not happened. The effectiveness of negative assurance is as dubious as the term suggests. It is patently more difficult to demonstrate, let alone interpret, a nonoccurrence than an occurrence. Occurrences of wrongdoing have the advantage of existing and therefore being detectable by the auditor. In order to be reassuring, then, the auditor must not actually find too many of them. There is an obvious tension here: if principals turn to audit primarily to confirm, rather than disconfirm, a positive view of the practices being audited, an audit has to be successful at detecting wrongdoing but not *too* successful.

Power thus compels us to see that the goal of an audit report has to be "essentially obscure." At its essence the goal of auditing is *both* to warn and to reassure, but since these are contradictory, the result is fundamental ambiguity.[19] Of course, auditors never announce that their product is ambiguous. But when pressed, all they can really say is that the practice in question gives a fair and true representation of itself. The point is this: an audit can never finally judge the practice itself, just the accuracy of the representation of the practice. *A church can never ultimately be deemed safe, merely that its systems tend to suggest safety.* Indeed, when auditors are accused of failing, they frequently abjure that clean audit reports can be produced even of companies that collapse. They are forced to admit that their opinion was essentially empty of concretely reassuring substance. This should be cold comfort for those who asked for the audit. Such a defense implies that the problem was one of false expectations, but this only begs the question of what people can expect from audits in the first place!

We have demonstrated some of the problematic features of audit. Given these problems, audits sometimes fail. That is, they fail to predict financial ruin, prevent or even detect misconduct, or ensure good practice. This should not surprise anyone who considers carefully the idea of audit, but interestingly enough, audit failure does continue to surprise the general public. They have come to believe that auditing works. "The role that is shaped for and demanded of auditing may only have a slender relation to its technical capabilities,"[20] yet confidence in audit is hard to shake. While on one level people may acknowledge that they can only do so much background checking before it becomes unfeasible, and thus cannot rely on this strategy for preventing misconduct, they nevertheless continue to recommend background checks. That people cling to their confidence in the idea of audit is evident in recent cases of outright audit failure in the financial world: when an audit is irrevocably proven to have failed, as when fraud is subsequently revealed by a whistle blower, the public demands that someone look into the practices of the auditor. Rather than give up on the idea of audit, they call for an audit of the auditor! The process simply regresses and audits of ever-higher orders are created.

THE DANGERS OF BECOMING AN AUDIT SOCIETY

Let us consider some of the dangers that accompany the audit explosion. First of all, once practitioners start to be audited, their time and energy can shift from the practice itself to the work of making their practice auditable. A great deal of effort must go into packaging and presenting their work and bringing it in line with predetermined parameters of quality. Critics have called this "McDonaldization"—the ubiquitous standardization of professional practice—and argue that it distracts professionals and also imbues professional life with commercial values.[21] The effort to become auditable absorbs valuable resources that might otherwise be poured directly into the work. It shifts the power from professionals to their managers and increases the depth of bureaucracy through which professionals must wade as they go about their work. In so doing, the danger is that professionals will increasingly "settle" for externally imposed standards of good practice. This is worrisome for ministry given that we find ourselves in an age when creativity and fresh thinking are sorely needed, not necessarily more standardized practice.

Another danger lies in the type of motivation audit inspires. Instead of devotion to the substance of their work, practitioners become burdened with the task of verifying its outcomes. As they adjust to this burden, their motivation shifts from pursuing excellent, accountable performance to compliance. The shift is subtle but real. "New motivational structures emerge as auditees develop strategies to cope with being audited: it is important to be seen to comply with performance measurement systems while retaining as much autonomy as possible."[22] We must question whether compliance in the ministry is our ultimate goal. (Is it more important to demonstrate that you have called the proper authorities on a child's behalf, or to make the call and then direct your energy toward caring for the child?) As we saw when defining trust, compliance is not necessarily the same thing as trustworthiness; it is merely compliance. Nor does it necessarily grow into trustworthiness. "But I'm doing what you asked of me" is surely not what a truster really wishes to hear. It neither provides the assurance sought nor helps to grow relationship.

Finally, audits tend to discourage, rather than promote, discourse about good conduct within an organization. Once a report is produced, conversation tends to cease. Members of the community breathe a sigh of relief and think: "We wanted to protect ourselves against the risk of harm, so we had an audit done. Now that things have been determined sound, what more do we need to talk about?" Likewise, practitioners go back to "business as usual" once that business has been stamped with approval. Audit reports rarely prod them to go back and question further their techniques and methods. (How many organizations adopt their sexual harassment policies at annual meeting and then put them on the shelf? How many church schools continue to train their teachers beyond the first mandatory meeting about rules and requirements?) Audits "do not invite or provoke public dialogue; they are not designed to support public debate. . . . They do not so much communicate as 'give off' information by virtue of a rhetoric of 'neutrality, objectivity, dispassion, expertise.'"[23] In short, a further drawback to the idea of audit is that its goal is comfort rather than communication.[24] So while audits are often prompted by perceived or real problems in practice, their effect can ultimately be to discourage substantive improvement in that practice. This is a further irony of audit.

To summarize, audits and other "rituals of verification" are attractive, according to Power, because they appear to confirm our confidence in the work someone else is performing. They do this by examining samples of the work in question and verifying for us that these samples conform to our preestablished expectations. Unfortunately, despite our desire for assurance, and audits' seeming success in providing it, their attractiveness often ends there. The role audits play in sustaining confidence is ambiguous. If they help to confirm a positive view of a practitioner's work, then a positive view might have been unshakable to begin with. If audits succeed in help-ing performance line up with expectations, this may only beg the question of the propriety of the expectations in the first place. An audit can obscure the goals that ought to drive whatever work is being audited because it redirects people's attention to itself. In other words, the very requirements that go into making an audit succeed may ultimately cause deterioration of excellent work. Audits value process over content, consistency over variety, transparency over sophistication, risk aversion over risk taking, tidiness over complexity. The more audits are used, the further they entrench the former values and the more they put good practice at risk.

The audit explosion can be dangerous for trust but it also exposes the way trust has been poorly practiced in the past. "Overall the audit explo-sion has ambivalent implications for trust. On the one hand, there is the suggestion that audits create the distrust they presuppose and that this in turn leads to various organizational pathologies, if not 'fatal remedies'. . . . On the other hand, there is also a need to recognize a form of silly or naive trust which ignores the evidence of corporate history."[25]

THE NEED TO TRUST IN TRUST

Borrowed as it is from the worlds of management and finance, the forego-ing discussion may seem alien to the life of the church that is our interest. Yet I hope the analogies to and implications for ministry practice have at least been sketched. There are enough similarities between the practices of audit that Power describes and the misconduct prevention strategies in the church to warrant our concern that the church might be in danger of becoming an "audit society." Safe church policies and procedures enjoy current popularity for the same reasons audits do. They are perceived to be not only an overdue response to trouble—in this case a serious and embarrassing record of past abuse in the church—but also a way to pre-vent trouble in the future. Leaders in the church, not unlike leaders in the financial world, believe that if they can check up on conduct, they will be reassured that it is above reproach.

We can understand and even sympathize with the yearnings implicit in these attempts to do something to make the church safe. And yet we must question whether they are being overvalued. We have seen that, like audits, procedures to verify, regulate, and control ministerial conduct can backfire. Power's analysis of audit, both in concept and in practice, should give us pause. In any organization with a high level of complexity and freedom, risk can never be removed and conduct can never be entirely controlled. Thus, safety can never be completely assured. The church is no exception. Trustworthiness cannot be secured through rituals of verification there any more than in the financial world. As Onora O'Neill writes: "The possibility of being mistaken, deceived, and even betrayed cannot be written out of life."[26]

There is an even greater peril, however, than the probability that safe church measures will not work. It is this: attempts to secure trustworthiness can in the long run undermine the practice of trust itself. Ironic though it may seem, trying to replace traditional forms of trust with other methods of securing accountability and reliability actually threaten to endanger the former. Why should this be? The answer is that no community can finally dispense with trust altogether, so when new, competing practices appear to secure professional trustworthiness, the work of trust gets gradually ignored.

As we defined it earlier in this work, the practice of trust is one of accepting vulnerability to possible but unanticipated risk of harm. It requires continual assessment of possible harm, discernment about whether and when to be vulnerable, and discretion in trust's placement. This is hard work indeed, but there is no substitute for it so long as the potential for harm exists and at the same time, clergy are given a distinctive role in the church. While it may be possible for disillusioned members to cease trusting clergy and leave the church, it is not possible for members to stay in the church and not continue to trust their clergy and other leaders at least to some degree. The choice, in other words, is not between trust and distrust, but between bestowing trust carefully or misplacing it.[27]

In the audit society, however, this choice gets obscured. When people in a community come to rely on audits, it appears that they have decided not to trust and given in to distrust. That is, they appear to have given up on trying to discern for themselves whether or not their leaders are trustworthy and turned instead to outside sources for verification. Contrary to this assumption, however, communities that turn to audit are not necessarily distrusting but have simply transferred their trust. They transfer it from people to policies and procedures. "The audit society is only superficially a 'distrusting society'. Indeed, auditing is a practice which must be trusted and which is also itself, of necessity, trusting."[28] Indeed, people in "safe" churches do not really stop trusting. They just bestow their trust elsewhere, now to checking-up processes meant to ensure their safety.

The problem is that trusting policies and procedures may be misplaced trust. It cannot provide the same level of comfort. If the need for trust is born out of fear and anxiety, fear and anxiety may only be compounded as trust becomes diffused among impersonal systems. As O'Neill says, "The steps taken are designed to make trust less necessary; but the anxieties persist because trust is also less achievable."[29] Anxiety can be heard in the inquiries people start making about the reliability of the systems put in place to ensure reliability. Trust that has regressed to another level is not necessarily stronger or any more reassuring.

The corollary to misplaced trust is misplaced mistrust. In other words, audits can sometimes train us to mistrust the wrong people. As O'Neill points out, this problem is typically dubbed the problem of Cassandra, after the Greek mythological figure who was given the gift of prophecy but also the curse of being ignored. She raised her voice against potential danger but she was unfairly mistrusted. We must be careful here when talking about ministerial misconduct because the specter of false accusation is still overblown by those who continue to deny its existence. Nevertheless, safe church practices *can* exacerbate the Cassandra problem because in the process of searching for misconduct—even with the hope of proving it nonexistent—we might begin to suspect everyone. The distinction between the innocent and the potentially guilty gets blurred, and this can cause unnecessary trouble for everyone.

> Cassandra's problem is neither the best, nor the worst of life's possibilities. Trust placed unsuspectingly in untrustworthy agents and institutions that deceive and betray that trust is worse. Yet mistrust directed inaccurately at trustworthy persons and institutions also leads to unnecessary anxiety (for the needlessly mistrusting) and to grief and difficulties (for the needlessly mistrusted).[30]

Sometimes we just need to trust trust.[31] This is what audits derail. By automatically demanding an immediate account from trustworthy and untrustworthy alike, they fool us into believing we no longer have to figure out for ourselves when to demand an accounting, or, conversely, when it may be better to delay interrogation for a while. We forget how to decide when it is sound to enter into a trust relationship, and when the relationship might have to end. Over time they weaken the powers of discernment that are so central to trust. This can be dangerous. So, how can the church practice smarter trust and still make itself safer? We return to the lessons about trust that we have learned.

SMARTER TRUST AND SAFER CHURCHES

First, since ministerial misconduct puts the most vulnerable at risk of the most harm, trust relationships in a "safe" church must be carefully established. No one should be put at more risk than is appropriate. Programs and activities should be carefully planned and safe contexts arranged. Many of the guidelines listed earlier, such as the two-adult rule, are helpful not only because they reduce risk but also because they make everyone more conscious of the trust relationships that exist between leaders and followers. This is especially true if the guidelines are implemented in the context of a comprehensive education program aimed at fostering a culture of mutual accountability and empowerment.

Second, it would probably be better if we stopped using the term "safe church" and substituted "safer." Just as sexuality educators at one point switched from the term "safe sex" to "safer sex" because they realized that the former promoted false hopes in the effectiveness of sexually transmitted disease prevention measures, we should probably cease to imply that churches can be made 100 percent safe. People in a "safer" church would be aware of the fact that to trust each other will inevitably involve a certain amount of risk. Instead of denying the risks, they would openly acknowledge them while at the same time trying to minimize them.

Admittedly, we said in chapter 1 that partners to a trust relationship can only say to each other "I'm trusting you, remember" so many times before the trust is effectively killed. But we also said that transparency generally supports trust. I suspect that most parishioners could stand to be more transparent about the ways they trust each other before this danger were run. Even something as simple as getting to know the leaders of various church programs helps to make a trust relationship explicit and therefore stronger.[32] To continue the analogy, sexuality educators have said that even when employing preventive measures, nothing substitutes for direct, personal communication between parties who are in a relationship together.

The act of holding one another accountable to standards of good conduct can be very powerful. Again, this does not have to mean a nagging reminder from Persons A that they are keeping a vigilant eye on Persons B. Mutual accountability can take many forms. Often rituals are helpful. Many groups find that writing a code or covenant of behavior together keeps them in mind of the ways they want to treat each other.[33] A common practice in small group ministry is to establish guidelines for respectful conversation, and to repeat them at the start of every meeting. In the tradition of faith-based organizing that many congregations have learned, an evaluation concludes every single gathering, with leaders and followers alike critiquing each other's participation in the event that has just taken place. These and other sorts of rituals of accountability must be practiced consistently every time people come together to be in relationship, not just when problems arise. That way, relationship building becomes part of the fabric of community life and people do not find themselves only responding to misconduct, but to good conduct as well. These sorts of rituals serve, in effect, as symbols of the community's repeated, deliberate, chosen act of establishing and reestablishing trust.

Safer churches are also communities where roles are carefully outlined and communicated. Trust between persons in workplace settings is greatly aided by role clarification. In fact, few conditions contribute to foolhardy trust more than misunderstandings about what people can expect from each other. To use an analogy from government, Annette Baier points out that those who govern our land receive help defining their roles from the U.S. Constitution. Legislators, judges, and presidents know—at least in theory—where their sphere begins and ends because the Constitution establishes a balance among the three spheres. Compared to citizens of some other nation-states, the American public is relieved of having to rely entirely upon the individual characters of the people in power because we have put certain temptations outside of the reach of their role. "Amendments such as the Twenty-second, limiting presidential terms to two, show proper fear of the abuses that prolonged power would make tempting to a president."[34] Churches can take a cue from constitutional designs. I am not necessarily saying that churches ought to have constitutions, but, rather, that they would benefit from a better understanding of the relative functions of ministers, staff, volunteers, deacons—not to mention bishops, presidents, and so forth. Understanding who is held accountable for what ministries prevents confusion and alleviates the pressure of the clergy role. It would help clarify *what* a minister is to be entrusted *with* and thus make trust a little easier.

Studies have shown, moreover, that ministerial misconduct is often related to role confusion, that is, when ministers step beyond their boundaries. Clearly a full discussion of this problem is beyond the scope of this book, but suffice it to say that clergy and laypeople alike would greatly benefit from conversation about where the clergy's role in the church begins and where it is taken up by others. Church people also need together to discern whether ministry and romance are compatible, and even how the roles of minister and friend relate. These role crossings lead to the most confusion. In short, holding one another accountable becomes easier when all agree on the scope of what behavior is to be held to account. As Annette Baier writes: "So even if we lack any useful rules for individuals on when to give and when to withhold trust, we are not entirely without guidelines on how to design roles for individuals that will help them avoid the worst forms of untrustworthiness, or of oppressively burdensome trust, or of overly vulnerable trusting."[35]

Finally, safer churches not only acknowledge the possibility of risk of harm but also know how they will respond when harm occurs. As counter-intuitive as it may sound, one way to minimize the risk of harm is to be ready for it. Faith communities are reassured when they have developed a disciplinary procedure for misconduct, much the way coastal dwellers are reassured by the evacuation plan they will follow in the event of a hurricane. Adopting a response plan for misconduct also communicates a clear message that the community will not tolerate it. This alone creates a climate of reassurance, for people can trust each other to face misconduct squarely and not look the other way. Unlike the verification procedures discussed above, disciplinary procedures are not employed until they are needed, but they are created ahead of time. If well communicated and disseminated, their very existence thus serves as both a warning to potential abusers and a comfort to potential victims.

In fact, I believe that disciplinary procedures often do even more to prevent misconduct than other approaches to risk reduction. This is especially true because ministerial misconduct nearly always takes place within the context of a trust relationship that has an imbalance of power. A minister always has power over a parishioner, if only the power of their ordained role. Laypeople in special positions of responsibility also carry power. Anyone in a unique position to offer help because of their position and expertise can exercise power over the vulnerable persons who turn to them. Therefore, ministerial misconduct does not just cause pain, it also abuses power. Unfortunately, there is little we can do to change the power differential in a ministerial relationship. This makes it all the more important to guard trust in other ways. Disciplinary action is one of these ways. It offsets the imbalance of power between Person A and Person B by bringing in the collective power of the community on Person A's behalf.

Annette Baier argues that the presence of a reliable procedure for disciplining wrongdoers cannot be underestimated. It does nothing less than rearrange the entire institutional design. Having ombudsmen and institutional complaint procedures in mind, she compares the effect of discipline to that of appeals courts: lower-court judges become more careful. She argues that discipline procedures work not so much by inciting fear among would-be abusers, but also by reducing the very possibility of getting away with abuse and thus the temptation to it. Well-designed procedures, she says, actually "mold people to make them more trustworthy."[36]

A community that stands ready and willing to take disciplinary action against perpetrators of misconduct effectively promises potential victims that any breach of their trust will result in an end to the relationship. The community, along with the victim, becomes the body who discerns whether a trust relationship must end. To take disciplinary action against someone who has committed misconduct is to say that the trust relationship has been broken by one of the parties, and is now over. Discipline makes clear that trust does not necessarily last forever nor is it endlessly flexible. Trust—at least the kind we are talking about in this book—follows certain conditions. It is not unconditional. Therefore, there is no contradiction between trust and discipline. On the contrary, ending a trust relationship that was once entered in good faith is healthier than perpetrating a sense of distrust. It is an honest and straightforward action. It is a way of honoring the truster and, even, the trust relationship that once existed.

Unfortunately, the church has not always lifted up discipline as a virtue! We are much more inclined to talk about forgiveness. While a full discussion of the ethics of forgiveness is not possible here, it should be pointed out that sometimes an unreflective rhetoric of Christian forgiveness contributes to the faith community's insufficient response to misconduct. An emphasis on the value of forgiveness is consistent with the "therapeutic model" of ministry we spoke of in chapter 2. Many people are convinced that the practice of forgiveness has therapeutic value for both victim and perpetrator and thus urge victims to learn eventually how to forgive. They also tend to interpret forgiveness in psychological rather than moral terms, preferring to talk about growth and healing rather than absolution for sin. One writer says that "psychologically conscious parishioners are likely to prefer psychological language and concepts for dealing with moral concerns, including forgiveness, over traditional and moral categories and terminology, for better or for worse—though I think it is some of both."[37] Thus, it becomes doubly difficult for those dealing with misconduct to get others to accept the notion of disciplining a ministerial leader by, say, removing or suspending them from ministry practice. "I suppose we should keep them on because as Christians we're called to forgive," I heard someone recently say. But as one of the premier experts on misconduct prevention, Marie Fortune, writes: "Forgiveness on the part of victims of violation becomes an option if some sort of justice has been done on their behalf."[38] In other words, a firm moral response to misconduct must precede any call for forgiveness. The two are not only not contradictory but inseparable.

Christian communities can be too forgiving as well as too trusting. Both serve to undermine trustworthiness in the long run. While Christians may be better known for their forgiveness, it may be the ability to judge whether it is time to forgive—or not—that serves us just as well. Baier could have been writing about the Christian community when she wrote of how proper forgiveness establishes a network of trust: "Unforgiving rigidity and, at the other extreme, easygoing willingness to keep on forgiving are both dysfunctional weaknesses, if our goal is to maintain and repair a network of beneficial trust, one composed of normally faulty human persons."[39] The church maintains itself as a network of trust by teaching its members—"normally faulty human persons" all of us—how to practice *both* forgiveness *and* admonishment. In a healthy church community, members hold one another accountable for their behavior. They are not unwilling to call each other to account when necessary.

In the end, to return to the question with which we began, checking up on leaders will not necessarily make them more trustworthy. It is trustworthy institutions that nurture trustworthy leaders. And "trustworthy institutions will be those that distribute power in such a way that [corruption by power] is less likely."[40] Institutions where power is as evenly distributed as possible and where vigilance is exercised to keep it that way, are the places where you will find leaders who can be entrusted with the power that comes with their role. Indeed, the most hopeful sign of trustworthiness in a leader may be when she consistently seeks ways to empower others, thus distributing even her own power throughout the community.

In conclusion, we have argued in this book that the dynamics of trust are delicate. The desire to reduce the risk of misconduct has arisen in the church in part precisely because people in the church have in the past overextended it. One author writes:

> Unfortunately, the church is among the last institutions to respond to this crisis [of child sexual abuse]. There are a number of reasons for this: We are too trusting. We come to church to be spiritually renewed, to feel

a part of community. We feel safe in this environment. We find it hard to imagine that some in our spiritual community would betray others.[41]

It is indeed possible to be too trusting. And yet it is equally possible to become too distrusting. Our ultimate goal is not to replace trust with distrust or with trust in procedures but to practice smarter trust in each other. When we do so, we will still be able to come to church to be spiritually renewed, to feel part of a community, and to be in an environment that fees safe.

Chapter Four

৯ GOSSIP

Amy: (observing Chris walk to the parking lot after church, kids in tow who are hitting each other): Chris sure has a handful with those kids.

Barb: Yeah, and to imagine that she homeschools them and has to be with them 24-7!

Amy: I would never be able to homeschool my kids.

Barb: Me, neither. I love 'em dearly, but I don't mind seeing them board the bus some mornings. I wonder if her husband helps out much.

Amy: I shouldn't say this, but I've always thought he was a little odd. You know, in terms of social skills. . . . maybe he was homeschooled himself!

Amy and Barb: (laugh)

৯ ৯ ৯

Amy: (observing Chris walk to the parking lot after church, kids in tow who are hitting each other): Chris sure has her handful with those kids.

Barb: Yeah, I would think she'd need a break from them. You know, she homeschools them so she's with them 24-7.

Amy: I would never be able to homeschool mine. I wonder how it affects your relationship with your kids. Do you know many other homeschooling families?

Barb: No one else that I know very well. I think maybe Dena does. And, you know, our church was asked to lend Sunday school room space during the week to a group that homeschools.

Amy: Well, that would be interesting, seeing as our pastor's husband is superintendent of the schools. I've always supported the public schools, but it seems like some people really believe in this homeschooling business.

ᔑ ᔑ ᔑ

Chris: My name is Chris, and I've been a member of this church for three years. I grew up in another denomination, but I switched to this one when I moved here and found this church. From the very first Sunday I attended, I have known this to be a friendly and supportive congregation. I have three small children, ages 8, 5, and 3. I love being a mother, but I will admit that at times they are a handful and I feel overwhelmed. My husband and I also homeschool them, sharing that responsibility as much as we can although he has a full-time job at the university. We are glad that our kids are growing up in this church. They love Sunday school and singing in the junior choir, and as you all probably know, they are enthusiastic participants at coffee hour, especially when there are chocolate chip cookies! My husband and I are enjoying Wednesday Evening Bible Study and learning a lot there. He never went to church before this, and he can be shy at times because he's still getting used to what it means to be a church member, and he readily admits he doesn't know the Bible at all! I have gone to church my whole life, so I feel more at ease in church, but I must say this is the first time I have studied the Bible carefully, the way we do it here. I've discovered a lot about it that I never knew before. Reading the Psalms, especially, has been wonderful. I think it has changed the way I pray to God and has made my faith stronger. That's just one reason I am thankful for this church and why I wanted to give my testimony today.

Gossip is a natural form of human communication. It occurs whenever curiosity about somebody exceeds the information available about them. When people are interested or want to understand better their fellow human beings, they share whatever information they can.[1] When members of a community care about one other and want to know more about each other, they talk. *They share bits of information about others that they have gleaned from sundry sources. They speculate on the meaning and implications of this information, perhaps even on its veracity. They offer their opinions, positive and negative, about what they have heard. They comment on and evaluate the person being talked about and often add color and interest to the story. In short, they gossip. By gossiping, community members express their concern for one another, because by talking about somebody who is not present, they effectively draw that person more closely into their fold. Gossip shows that you are interested in others' well-being. Not to care about personal information is not to care about a person. Gossip is a form of care.*

Gossip is thus especially fitting in church. Church members aspire to care about one another and to probe beyond the barriers of privacy so quickly erected in secular society. Parishioners practice their own lay form of pastoral care by talking about each other. It is to be expected that they know intimate details about one another's lives, for this is the first step in helping each other out. Far from mere curiosity, this interest is the way parishioners sustain one another in prayer and loving action.

Particularly in small communities, gossip usually gets back to its target, the person whose goings-on have been the subject of talk. Frequently, this is the intention of the gossipers, however implicit. They know that the sharing of information, along with its layers of commentary and evaluation, will eventually wind its way back to the target. But since such communication is indirect, with the precision blurred of who precisely said precisely what, it can be a gentle way to receive commentary about oneself. One could even call it a more civil form of speech than direct communication. Gossip shows deference for its target by circumventing the bluntness and inevitable seriousness of face-to-face talk. Its light, sometimes even playful, quality softens the blow of any inaccurate or negative content.

Gossipees do not necessarily mind being gossiped about. They may even find it flattering. While those talked about may be disturbed to discover that false or personal information about them has been circulating, they may tolerate even these forms of gossip for the sake of being included in gossipers' circle. Gossip makes them feel worthy of other people's attention.

Gossip also serves to set and strengthen community standards. People often engage in gossip as a safe way to test what other people think about certain behaviors. Through the commentary that follows news about a third person, gossipers exchange their views. Gossip is, after all, very often about behaviors on the "edge," those that push the boundaries of socially accepted practice.

Gossipers can express their skepticism or, alternatively, their acceptance of the behavior at hand and in this way, refine or reestablish their community's norms.

§   §   §

This is the case made for gossip. As persuasive as it may be, in the end I do not accept it. Unlike its defenders, I do not think gossip contributes to the practice of trust within the faith community. In the rest of this chapter, I hope to show why. I will argue that if our aim is to support the growth of trust relationships, we should consider gossip an unhelpful practice for Christian communities and learn the practice of testimony instead. While the former does not foster trust, the latter can. But first we must establish a working definition of gossip.

GOSSIP DEFINED

Like many human actions, our moral evaluation of gossip depends heavily on how it is defined. Casual speculation on what the tabloids say about celebrities may be less reprehensible than a deliberately spread nasty rumor about a close friend. Some might even question whether either of these truly count as "gossip"—the former has so little chance of getting back to the target as to be practically harmless, and the latter is so intentionally mean it might better belong to the category of malice. If you are going to disapprove of gossip, it is important to define it fairly carefully, rather than simply assume everyone knows what you are talking about.

I opened this chapter with three vignettes of people speaking about the same thing to tease out the differences between what is gossip and what is not. In my view, the first constitutes gossip whereas the second does not, and the third is an example of testimony.

I define gossip as informal, evaluative discourse about someone not present who is a member of the speakers' social group. These features—the informality, the absence of the person being talked about, the evaluative or judgmental nature of the discourse, and the relational context—are ones I take to be necessary and sufficient features of gossip. I think this definition covers most instances of what most people would recognize as "gossip." But in reality, gossip is one of those phenomena with fuzzy definitional boundaries. It is probably best characterized as a prototype rather than a clear category.[2] Hence, most scholars of gossip refer to "typical" or "paradigmatic" cases, recognizing that there may be few "pure" ones.

In addition to the features I have already listed, then, I would add several more that usually, but not always, signify gossip. Typically, but not necessarily in every instance, gossip's subject matter is titillating. People use the phrase "a juicy bit of gossip" because they do not just find gossip interesting but particularly savor it. Sometimes it is called "spicy" or "hot." It can be a pleasurably messy activity to engage in, perhaps even a bit naughty. Usually, truth and falsity matter less than entertainment value when it comes to the specific content of gossip. Finally, when people gossip, they usually do not hold each other strictly accountable for what they say; gossip is understood to express the opinion of the moment. Gossipers also tend not to hold each other to strict confidentiality. They may say, "Now, don't repeat this, but . . . ." but not really mean it.

Let me return to my original, pared-down definition of gossip. Gossip is, first of all, an informal type of discourse. In contrast, "formal" discourse includes most published writing, public speaking, agreements and contracts and other communications with legal intent, and conversations between people who have public relationships to one another. Another way of saying that gossip is informal is to say that it is casual. As a form of conversation, it tends to arise spontaneously and without explicitly stated purpose. (We will see later, however, that gossip is not purposeless.) Proof of gossip's informality is found in the gossiper's defense when questioned about the propriety of their conversation. They will invariably demur, saying something like, "Oh, we don't mean anything by it," or "We're just having fun," or "chatting." Gossipers contend that gossip is fun, frequently humorous, a way to pass the time. In other words, they themselves deny that what they are doing should be taken too seriously.

While we may or may not want to accede to gossipers' description of gossip as nonserious (for, as we will see, it can have serious consequences), we can agree that it is not strenuous. Gossipers do not understand themselves to be debating the great questions of the day. It is not a kind of discourse that demands great mental effort. Few things, besides the subject showing up, kill gossip more effectively than someone who tries to turn it into a discussion. British scholar Gabriele Taylor writes that "it requires no abstract thought or the working out of political, ideological, or moral views."[3] This is why gossip has long been called "idle talk." Again, this characterization misses the importance of gossip in people's lives, but the point to be taken is that gossip is informal discourse. I will later show why I think its informality poses a danger to community.

Second, I define gossip as evaluative. In other words I do not take just any informal conversation about an absent third party to be gossip. This distinguishes my definition from others and from the way people often refer to gossip in ordinary parlance. If I am simply exchanging news of a recent engagement or birth or hospitalization, without adding evaluative commentary, I am not necessarily gossiping. When I add a judgment such as "I can't believe *those* two are going to tie the knot," or "I heard she didn't really want to have a third child but her husband wanted to try for a son," or "I bet he got diabetes because of his terrible eating habits," then I probably am. If I share information about a student on campus with my colleague so that he can anticipate what the student will need to do to graduate, I am not gossiping. But if I go out for martinis after class with that colleague and we place bets on which students will drop out by the end of the academic year, we are gossiping.

Naturally there is a fine line here, and people frequently take advantage of it even while sensing they may be crossing it. A student of mine once told me that her aunt fills her in on all the newsy tidbits from church when she returns home for visits. Each time, her aunt prefaces her news account by saying, "Now, this isn't gossip, but Christian concern." I suspect that if my student's aunt feels compelled to include such a disclaimer, even *she* must have a hunch that it is gossip she is sharing, not Christian concern. In the first vignette, above, Amy makes a joke about Chris's husband, indicating that she finds him somewhat antisocial. This judgmental comment is unnecessary to Amy's and Barb's concern about Chris. It is purely gratuitous and therefore, I think, moves their discourse into the category of gossip.

Third, gossip is a kind of discourse that takes place in the absence of its subject. Nearly everyone who writes about gossip agrees on this. While Sissela Bok entertains the notion that it is possible to participate in gossip about oneself, even she defines gossip in terms of the target's virtual, if not literal, absence.[4]

The target's absence makes possible certain other features of gossip. When you talk about someone who is not present, you can editorialize and speculate. You do not have to pay strict attention to accuracy but can "spice up" the story a bit, thereby making it more interesting and yourself a livelier conversation partner. Gossipers are known for playing fast and loose with the facts; others give them tacit acceptance especially when the gossipy context is made clear. With the target absent, gossipers can have some fun with information they share. If gossip is supposed to be pleasurable—if it satisfies our desire freely to probe hidden details of other people's lives—then the target *must* not in fact be present. It would not be nearly as much fun if she were to show up and make herself available for direct scrutiny. As literary theorist Patricia Meyer Spacks writes in her book, *Gossip*: "Gossip insists on its own frivolity."[5]

In this respect, we might compare gossip to voyeurism. Being a gossip is a bit like being a Peeping Tom: one gets to pry into the private spaces of people's lives. It shares the same kind of excitement: one enjoys a glimpse into forbidden territory without the subject finding out. This feature of gossip is also key to understanding why many have difficulty condemning gossip morally. Like voyeurism, it strikes many as a harmless, even victimless, crime. If the person being talked about is not there, how can it hurt? Most gossipers probably assume, or try to convince themselves of, the harmlessness of what they are doing.

With secrecy, as we have seen, there are often very good reasons to exclude others. One can even argue that there are instances where talking about someone in their absence is both necessary and harmless—such as when doctors discusses a patient's case with medical students as part of their education, or when camp counselors swap stories about the children at the end of the day just to let off steam, or when people question their friends about their lovers' behavior. But when the other features of gossip are added—the informality, the spiciness, the evaluation that goes on, the lack of concern for accuracy and confidentiality—we begin to see that these instances just named may not really be gossip at all, at least as I am defining it. Particulars of a patient's case may no longer be confidential, but accuracy is crucial and spiciness is hardly the concern. When camp counselors complain about their charges to one another, they may exaggerate their complaints in order to work up a proper belly-ache, but they usually abide by a rule of confidentiality—whatever is said in the counselors' cabin stays in the counselors' cabin and never gets repeated to supervisors or parents or other children. And when friends gather to talk about their love lives (à la *Sex and the City*), the talk may admittedly be both spicy and evaluative, but it stays informal, and therefore gossip, only so long as no real problems are discussed. When serious issues are shared among the group, the discourse is better called counsel than gossip.

Counsel describes what Amy and Barb are approaching in the second vignette, above. I would argue that here Amy displays genuine interest in understanding homeschooling, whereas in the first vignette, Amy and Barb seem tacitly to agree that homeschooling is not something people like them would ever consider, even that it is a bit weird. I define the first exchange as gossip but not the second. Because these exchanges do not differ greatly, we see that the definition of gossip rests not so much on subject matter but more on the intentions, assumptions, and attitudes reflected. As Taylor writes, "Gossiping is a pleasurable activity and is seen as such by those engaging in it. Their pleasurable interest gives gossip its particular 'feel.'"[6] The distinctive "feel" of gossip can also be sensed in its self-absorption. In the first vignette, Amy and Barb are likely "sussing" each other up about the propriety of homeschooling as a form of education, or about Chris as a church member, or about gender roles in marriage. (We would have to hear how their conversation proceeded to determine which.) They do not necessarily appear to have topmost in their minds the well-being of homeschoolers, Chris, or married couples. Their attitude is not really one of great curiosity or compassion directed outward toward Chris. The second vignette, in contrast, suggests an attitude of interest, if not concern, in a phenomenon new to their community and in a fellow member of their church. Amy and Barb are more actively engaged in trying to figure Chris out, or figure homeschooling parents out, and whether their church should support this novel form of education.

Finally, I argue that gossip is discourse shared among people in the same social group about others also in that group. I may enjoy reading about celebrities in what are called "gossip columns," but they are not in my social circle. Gossip columns are better categorized as entertainment designed to be sold for profit. They are part of an industry, not a form of communication (not that this justifies industrialists profiting from people's personal lives). Prototypical gossip is about friends by friends. Or about colleagues by colleagues, or about church members by other members. Gossip flourishes in the workplace because co-workers are curious about each other and their relative standing within the organization. The image of office workers swapping stories while standing around the water cooler is practically a trope for gossip. And, of course, fellow parishioners constitute a social group. Amy, Beth, and Chris are all members of the same church. (They even appear to be members of a subgroup within the church that does not include Dena.) Thus, Amy and Beth can easily exchange opinions about Chris and her family.

German sociologist Jörg Bergmann points out that the word *gossip* is both a noun and a verb, signifying, he argues, the inseparability of context from content. He calls gossip "news-for-a-social-unit" and gives an instructive example: "To take a classic gossip-theme, if a woman has an extramarital affair then we would surely call her friends' and neighbors' discussions about this event gossip, but not the injured husband's discussion of it with his divorce lawyer."[7] Within the right social unit, the news is considered gossip; in the wrong context, not.

To summarize, gossip is a very common form of speech that may be difficult to define precisely but, by its commonality, is something most of us would readily recognize. In other words, "we know it when we see it." Israeli philosopher Aaron Ben-Ze´ev offers us a fitting summary of it in the following statement. Although he defends gossip on moral grounds, I concur with his definition:

> Most people like to gossip now and then: it is a form of social commentary that usually revolves around information not yet widely known and therefore intriguing. The information generally concerns people who are not there to hear it, and includes both description and evaluation of their behavior. Participants appear to share the same standards of right and wrong. And although adherence to such standards is often superficial, even the mere appearance of common moral standards establishes intimacy among the participants.[8]

GOSSIP DEFENDED

Defenses of gossip do seem to abound. Bergmann thinks there is a "public rehabilitation" of gossip going on in both popular and academic literature.[9] I observed a similar trend some years ago among pastoral theologians who seemed to be interested in rehabilitating this practice. Let me describe three instances here. Richard Lischer, professor of homiletics at Duke Divinity School and author of *Open Secrets*, in a memoir of the years spent in his first parish as a Lutheran pastor, recalls how he worried at first about the level of gossip among his parishioners but eventually came to see it as essential to ministry. Gossip, he argues, is the way a community comes to grip with the unexpected or novel. Gossip gives them the means to process odd personalities and deviant behaviors. He cites the example of a crusty old parishioner who, one Sunday, rudely mocked the junior choir's performance of a new song. Shocked at his behavior, and thus thrown into pastoral crisis mode, Lischer had proposed to the elders after the service that they seek the man out and, with firm but loving concern, address what had happened. "He's hurting and confused. We have to work through this with him and resolve the issues involved."[10] The elders just looked at Lischer and told him there was no need for that; everybody knew that the man in question was a boor. The "crisis," Lischer realized, did not need to be handled head-on with pastoral sensitivity. The community knew how to deal with this man because they had gossiped about him for years. Eventually this very story about Lischer became part of the elders' gossip. It "was absorbed into the communal memory, mulched, and reprocessed for use in another form, perhaps as a joke, or a cautionary tale for future pastors . . ."[11]

The target of gossip had behaved disgracefully, so to turn the incident into a joke or cautionary tale rather than confront him directly, was, Lischer implies, in this case a gentle and proper response. The man deserved any expense he paid for being the community's target of gossip. Without the ability to gossip about each other, the parishioners in this very small town would simply have grown too weary of taking things on directly all the time. As an informal mode of discourse, gossip let them share information and come to unspoken consensus about each other's behavior without a lot of fuss.

In this vein, Lischer also shares a story of how his own wife became the target of gossip. Tracy was partway through a doctorate when she and Lischer moved to this small town in southern Illinois. A pastor's wife, housewife, and mother of two small children in addition to doctoral candidate, she had precious little time to work on her dissertation, so occasionally she would hire a babysitter to watch the children while she studied. Apparently, hiring a babysitter in order to sit in the backyard and read books was unorthodox behavior in this village. Gossip about her flew. In the end, reports Lischer, through gossiping, his parishioners came to "grudging appreciation" of Tracy's unique style of balancing wifehood, motherhood, and work.[12]

Gossip was, moreover, their way of reaching consensus about matters of communal concern. Gossip helped townspeople collectively decide "what constitutes decent farming, honorable business, tolerable preaching, or effective parenting. Gossip was our community's continuing education."[13] In effect, Lischer defines gossip as a theological practice of the church. He acknowledges that it did not in every instance function gently, and might not be such a useful mode of discourse in a place where people did not already have to put up constantly and intimately with each other. And yet he speaks glowingly of gossip as constructive, pastoral speech when shared within a baptized community.

Kathleen Norris, poet and writer of contemplative nonfiction, concurs with Lischer's positive assessment of gossip. In *Dakota: A Spiritual Geography*, she reminds her readers that the word *gossip* originated as a term for one who sponsors another for baptism. Meaning "akin to God," gossip suggested a spiritual kinship or relationship. The OED, she reminds us, traces the English word to the root words *God* and *sibling*.[14] Accordingly, Norris describes the gossip in her small town of Lemmon, South Dakota, as a godlike activity. In her chapter "The Holy Use of Gossip" she offers as an example the heartfelt classified ads people would submit to the local newspaper, thanking the town for helping with blood donations, charities, and benefits to relieve medical debt. Other examples she cites include her town's talk about a couple considering divorce, their clucking over another couple's public screaming matches, and their speculation about a son's grave and sudden illness.[15]

Writing as she is about denizens of a small town, Norris describes gossip as the glue that holds them together. Sharing each others' "business" is just a way for people who have always lived together, and likely always will, to keep tabs on each other. It demonstrates their interest and concern for fellow members. Privacy is not, after all, so highly valued in a small, tight-knit community, and its members reinforce their sense of familiarity with one another by keeping the information about each other flowing freely. Not to know the latest news about somebody is to feel out of touch and disconnected from the community.

Thus, Norris justifies gossip in part by arguing that much of the time, privacy is an overrated value. In small communities, privacy is also a near impossibility. Citizens of small towns understand that "you become public property" in a place where an outsider can immediately be spotted.[16] Thus, it is more difficult to have secrets in a small town. Each person's identity becomes a shared commodity, and gossip a vehicle for giving shape to it.

Norris also claims that gossip targets one and all in equal measure. Gossip, she argues, "is essentially democratic."[17] Everyone from plumber to banker gets discussed. Democracy also dictates its content: all news, both positive and negative, benign and scandalous, trivial and weighty, is grist for the gossip mill. Indeed, Norris's examples of gossip range from tidbits in the paper's social column to rumors about death and divorce, suggesting that the gossip in her town will target everybody at one time or another. Hence, gossip serves a bonding function. "And although there are always those who take delight in the misfortunes of others, and relish a juicy story at the expense of truth and others' feelings, this may be the exception rather than the rule. Surprisingly often, gossip is the way small-town people express solidarity."[18]

Like Lischer, Norris can at times wax quite eloquent about gossip. As a reader, one can tend to forget that she is writing about stories swapped over the backyard fence, information passed casually between folks in the line at the grocery store. Gossip appears to claim new dimensions in her experience:

> Like the desert tales that monks have used for centuries as a basis for theology and way of life, the tales of small-town gossip are often morally instructive, illustrating the ways ordinary people survive the worst that happens to them; or, conversely, the ways in which self-pity, anger, and despair can overwhelm and destroy them. Gossip is theology translated into experience. In it we hear great stories of conversion, like the drunk who turns his or her life around, as well as stories of failure. We can see that pride really does go before a fall, and that hope is essential. We watch closely those who retire, or lose a spouse, lest they lose interest in living. When we gossip we are also praying, not only for them but for ourselves.[19]

If gossip's uses are really this, they are holy indeed.

A final defender of gossip I will cite here is pastoral theologian William Willimon. He shares the opinion that gossip is not only not bad, but a positive good for church communities. "Gossip, as a church activity without malice, may well be, at its best, the moral casuistry of ordinary people, a primary means of congregational bonding, a source of utterly essential moral data about ourselves, an everyday means of investigating communally what it means to be baptized."[20] Willimon, who, as we have seen, invites us to imagine a new ethic of confidentiality and privacy for the church, likewise encourages us to gossip. He believes that gossip is another extension of "going public" with our lives. In the church we are not (or should not be) strangers to one another. He argues that "in a church, as in a marriage, we aspire to be the sort of people who know a great deal of very personal information about one another without using that information to destroy one another."[21] Willimon goes so far as to criticize congregations where members do not know each other well enough to gossip about each other.

Willimon explains how, as a pastor, he would rely on gossip to aid his ministry of pastoral care. Having heard parishioners in his congregation gossip about a couple with marital problems, for example, he would pay a pastoral visit to the couple and simply present them with what he had heard. After getting past their irritation at being the latest subject of "the church rumor mill," most of the time, he claims, such parishioners would end up expressing gratitude for their community's support. They would usually confirm the truth of the gossip Willimon had heard, and they would ultimately be grateful for the community's intervention into their lives. In short, they would come to agree with his own interpretation of gossip as "the genuine concern of some fellow Christians" who cared about them but were not sure how to show it.[22]

Underlying Willimon's defense of gossip is clearly the conviction that, most of the time, its content is not only accurate but also disseminated innocently. He assumes that people share secrets not out of a desire to hurt one another but to share the burden of them. Furthermore, he obviously has in mind church communities wherein the members all know one another pretty well. "After all, it is a risky business to tell our deep secrets to perfect strangers. But that is not our situation in the church." Such assumptions may only beg the question of his definition of gossip; it may be that he is talking about speech that we would not recognize as such. After all, the parishioner approaching the ordained professional leader— that is, the pastor—to share information that might help the pastor do his job might not bear much resemblance to the type of talking behind people's back that we have been addressing. Nevertheless, Willimon calls it gossip rather than advising or consulting. He acknowledges that as a pastor he is tapping into traditional rituals of talking behind people's back. He clearly understands gossip to be informal, evaluative conversation about people who are absent but he chooses to sanctify, rather than discourage, its practice in the church.

In the small towns that Lischer and Norris conjure for us and the parishes Willimon envisions, people's lives are not solely their own but in a sense common property. The meanings of what is public and what is private are blurred in a context of intimate relationships developed over a long time, and hence, gossip serves the purposes we have heard cited now three times: communal bonding, moral evaluation, and education.

GOSSIP STUDIED

Do studies of actual gossip habits support this rosy picture of it? While sociologists and psychologists tend not to make moral judgments about the behavior they investigate, for this is not their aim, their work can nevertheless shed informative light on our ethical task. Studies of gossip can help us answer the questions of who gossips about whom, what people are really doing when they gossip, and what appear to be their purposes in engaging in it. It is to the actual functioning of gossip within human communities, therefore, we now turn.

There are three things most researchers who have studied gossip say about it. The first thing they say, with which we can already concur, is that gossip is difficult to define. "Gossip is a slippery subject. Everyone seems to know what everyone else means by gossip except the researchers who have wrestled with it as a technical term."[23] The second thing they say about the subject of gossip is that it is understudied. "Until recently, philosophers and social scientists have paid scant attention to gossip."[24] They are fond of pointing out the ironic contrast between the apparent ubiquity of gossip in everyday human life and silence about it in scholarly literature. As a mode of discourse, it may be popular, but as a research topic, apparently it is not. Finally, researchers often say that gossip is by nature difficult to study (which is probably related to its unpopularity among them). Its informality and secrecy render formal investigation by a third party difficult. And yet, informal means of investigation that might catch people actually gossiping—hidden microphones and eavesdropping, for example—are dubious on both empirical and ethical grounds. As difficult they may be to come by, however, empirical results of research on gossip prove particularly valuable to us. If researchers are to be trusted, this informal, democratic, "idle" human activity is actually quite structured, purposeful, and revealing.

We have seen that pastoral theologians suggest the following community functions of gossip: social bonding, moral evaluation, and education or formation. Are these functions borne out in research? As it turns out, the answer is yes. But this does not necessarily mean we should encourage or even approve of the practice. *Just because gossip serves these functions does not necessarily mean that it builds trust.* People can bond together in tight groups that exclude others, their moral judgments can turn into moralizing, and "formation" can simply mean reifying the terms of what is socially acceptable. These practices do not necessarily build trust. In the end, then, whatever functions we might find gossip serves, we still seek an answer to our own distinct question: Does gossip contribute to or hinder the practice of trust within the faith community?

In order to answer this question, let us revisit the themes that we have come to associate with trust. We argued in chapter 1 that trust is always associated with risk, vulnerability, and power. Let us examine what the empirical studies tell us about the relationship of gossip to each of these factors.

Risk

Learning to practice trust well involves learning to accept an appropriate level of risk in our relationships with those we want or need to trust. Gossip, too, is associated with risk. At the very least, gossipers have to consider the risk of passing on information that might or might not be true about someone who might or might not find out. Thus, we are inclined to ask whether the sort of risk taking associated with gossip is the sort that will build trust. Is it true, as the pastoral theologians suggest, that people go out on a limb to talk about each other in order to care for one another? Or, as targets, do they risk being talked about inaccurately for the sake of being cared for?

We have posited that trust relationships are triadic in nature: Person A entrusts Person B with Valued Thing C. Interestingly enough, it turns out that gossip is similarly triadic. Prototypical gossip, as we have seen, has one person sharing information to a second about a third. In his fascinating and often amusing sociological study of gossip in Germany, Jörg Bergmann gives names to the characters in the gossip triangle. He calls them the gossip producer, the gossip recipient, and the subject of gossip.[25] (In other studies, the first and third are usually simply called the gossiper and the target.) Bergmann traces the noun *gossip*, that is, his gossip producer, back to its etiological root *god sib*, with which we are familiar from Norris. The God sibling was one who had access to intimate knowledge within the familial or social group; likewise, today's gossip is one who possesses knowledge of the private affairs of others. Since knowledge of this kind is almost always unevenly distributed among members of a social group, this makes the gossip producer a privileged person. For Bergmann, privileged access to private information renders the producer's information "contaminated."[26] The producer must therefore take care with its dissemination, as one would with any contaminated or toxic substance. He must choose with care who will receive his news. The gossip recipient, for his part, Bergmann argues, is "by no means merely a passive participant"[27] but, rather, someone who necessarily knows both the producer and the subject and is chosen to receive the information by virtue of his openness to hearing it and his potential as a future producer. When the information is passed between them, the producer and the recipient are joined in a special relationship by virtue of their shared knowledge. Bergmann likens it to the relationship between partners in crime. The recipient "finds himself, as it were, in the situation of one who accepts a gift that he as well as the giver knows is stolen."[28]

If Bergmann's characterization of the gossip relationship is at all accurate, then we must admit that it bears an uncanny resemblance to the trust relationship. Person A and Person B are bound together in a mutual agreement over Valued Thing C. The resemblance, however, stops there. For with gossip, the thing valued is not A's to begin with but, rather, something borrowed without permission, if you will, from Person C.

And thus the risk involved is different as well. Gossip may implicate Person A and Person B, but Person C does not get a say. What kind of risk do A and B take? Bergmann recorded, transcribed, and analyzed gossip conversations among residents of a housing development and discovered, after studying the transcripts, that gossip typically follows very careful linguistic patterns. There is what linguists call the "presequence," or hint from the producer that she has gossip to share and wants to test the recipient's readiness to hear it.[29] For example, she could say, "I guess the committee assignments were handed out . . . ," to which someone else could take the bait which would lead to gossip, or, alternatively, simply say "Yes, I guess so," and change the subject. Sometimes there is an "invitation" to talk issued by the recipient, a sort of "fishing expedition" to elicit suspected information.[30] "So, you were out late last night!" might be an example of a fishing expedition. Expressions of skepticism, amazement, and mock denial are additional techniques used to sound out and draw out the producer (such as, "You've *got* to be kidding!") The one seeking gossip may also toss out a speculative statement to see whether it gets confirmed, as in "I hear that . . ." (With conversationalists who know each other well, the process of initiating gossip is even easier. In the case of Bergmann's residents, there was a neighborhood store called the Pelster that served as a marketplace for gossip as well as groceries. All it took to get gossip going was for someone to ask casually, "What's new with the Pelster?"[31]) Finally, there are techniques used in telling the gossip story that the producer may use to exaggerate and embellish his content; he may insert claims to truthfulness to appear more believable; and he may add commentary and a tagline confirming that the story represents a general characteristic of the gossip subject ("And she's always doing things like that."). On the other hand, he may also (pretend to) hesitate to protect himself against appearing malicious ("I don't really want to say anything bad about someone else, but . . .").[32]

The point of all these linguistic devices, according to Bergmann, is to protect the gossipers from the risk associated with exchanging contaminated information. Bergmann believes that people know that gossip is morally condemnable; thus, if they want to gossip they have to appear as though they do not want to. Even from our own everyday experience, we know that gossipers frequently protect themselves by swearing their gossip partners to secrecy ("Now don't repeat this, but . . . ," or, even more baldly, "Now you didn't get this from me, but . . ."). As co-collaborators in a risky activity, producer A and recipient B must decide how deeply they want to be in relationship. For example, there is the "problem of making sure that the socially condemned practice of gossiping is shared by all the participants because this is the only way in which the gossip producer can avoid the unpleasant and fatal situation of appearing as the only one who is gossiping."[33] Bergmann believes that the primary risk of gossip, in other words, is of participating in a practice that society condemns.

Suppose we were to counter that not all "societies" condemn the practice of gossip. Is it not possible that some communities, like parishes, tacitly accept the practice of gossip and do not view its content as contaminated, as, say, Willimon argues? Might not some members view it as the next best thing to offering care in person? If this were the case, the risk of gossip would be minimal. Producers and recipients of gossip would not have to defend or deny or camouflage what they were doing. Furthermore, if gossip were not a condemned activity, we would expect everyone in the community to gossip about everyone in equal measure, or at least about everyone to the extent that everyone's activities were newsworthy. It would be, as Norris says, a democratic activity. Does the research support the contention that gossip is egalitarian and thus exposes everyone to the same risk?

On the contrary. For one thing, ordinary experience shows that people *do* defend and deny and camouflage their gossip behavior, as we have just seen, and therefore must consider it at least somewhat risky. Beyond that, everyone who conducts empirical studies of gossip finds that it is unevenly distributed within a community. In other words, members of a community never appear to gossip in equal measure nor do they all gossip in the same way. Rather, some members inevitably gossip far more than others and some gossip little. There are always some who gossip more gently, and others more viciously. Some try harder to preface their gossip with disclaimers; some repeat whatever they hear whether they really believe it or not. In other words, when it comes to gossip, not all members of a community situate themselves equally with respect to its practice. The gossipers, gossip receivers, and gossip targets within a social group are, as one social psychologist put it, "distinct and contrasting roles."[34]

Randall Young studied the gossip habits of over fifty sorority sisters in a college in California. In the first phase of his study he had the sisters answer a questionnaire about which among them were the most likeable, popular, and so forth, and also which ones gossiped the most and how critically (for example, "How much do you think _____ gossips about you in a flattering manner?").[35] In the second phase, he invited them to make up nicknames and tell stories about their sisters, in pairs, in a laboratory setting.

The results produced clear differentiations among the sisters. Gossip targets were, in short, the least-liked sisters. They enjoyed less admirable reputations and were known, as Young put it, for behaviors that were "noteworthy, but inappropriate."[36] They got teased more than other sisters. In the laboratory sessions, Young found that gossip about targets was less praiseworthy and harsher. "Participants telling stories about those who are normally targets of gossip were particularly dominant in their gossip behavior. There is not much risk involved in gossiping about those who normally get gossiped about, and the available fodder for negative information is presumably higher."[37] When targets themselves gossiped about their sisters, they were found to do so much less critically and with more indicators of politeness and deference. Young concluded that targets knew they were targets and acted accordingly. Gossip receivers, in contrast, were known and liked and had good reputations within the sorority. When gossiped about, the content was generally more positive. They were teased less, and teased playfully.[38] When receivers engaged in gossip themselves, they apologized less and appeared to feel free to be critical (although according to the questionnaires, they enjoyed a reputation of being gentle gossipers).[39]

What becomes clear from Young's data is that gossip patterns within a close-knit community (such as a sorority, and by analogy a parish) tend to reflect social status—and probably reinforce it, as well. Gossip does not appear to be a great equalizer. That the patterns of gossip activity tend to reflect and maintain existing social patterns is supported by another study carried out by a group of psychologists. Like Young, this team conducted its research, which consisted of administering questionnaires, with college sorority sisters. From initial information gleaned about friendship groupings, they drew a "map" of the sorority relationships. (The technical term for such a map is a sociogram; it resembles a constellation, with individuals as stars connected by one- or two-way arrows.) Then they asked about gossip patterns and, from these results, superimposed upon their map a set of arrows indicating who gossiped about whom. In addition, they administered a test measuring each woman's level of desire for social approval. Once again, it was found that targets of gossip were the least likable but also less needy of approval.[40] They discovered a few sisters who rarely gossiped at all; these same women had fewer friends than the rest. Perhaps most interesting was their finding that a cluster of sisters at the "knottiest" point of the sociogram constellation was also the most gossiped about and the most frequent gossipers. (Two women, in particular, had six or more arrows pointing in their direction, as compared to the more typical one or two.) The research team later discovered that "this clique appeared to contain the 'movers and shakers,' that is, the more active and influential sisters in the sorority."[41]

Thus, it appears that while gossip may be risky, as evidenced in the differentiation between those who indulge it and those who shy away, it is not necessarily risk that deepens or changes relationship. Nor is it some sort of social adhesive, at least not one evenly applied. Gossip may bond the popular members together but it appears to keep marginalized members at the margin rather than move them to the center. Indeed, social scientists have long hypothesized that far from serving as mere entertainment, gossip fulfills important social functions. These include social control, that is, establishing the boundaries between the insiders and outsiders of a social group. One sociologist described gossip this way: "Gossiping could be considered a laboratory case for the study of the construction of social relationships, of the drawing of boundaries between a We and a They, of the creation of moral solidarities, and of shifting alignments."[42] This is to say that if gossip bonds communities together, as some pastoral theologians are fond of claiming, it is perhaps not the mutual, egalitarian sort of bonding they imply. It is, rather, bonding through exclusion and the establishment of hierarchies among people. This may be "trust" of a certain sort but not the kind we wish to promote.

One might wish instead to argue that gossip facilitates interpersonal trust by clarifying the community's moral expectations in a low-risk manner. Gossip can communicate moral norms in ways that are indirect and subtle rather than direct and overbearing. Through gossip, individuals can test the waters of what the larger community deems morally acceptable and unacceptable. It could be argued that gossip allows us to talk about someone else's behavior as a pretext for concern about our own, thus letting us find out what our friends think about a particular topic in a safe, noncommittal manner. "It is of course much easier to participate vicariously in another's life than to struggle with one's own. Vicarious living has the added attraction of presenting a story the development of which one can take an interest in and speculate about, secure in the knowledge that it cannot adversely affect oneself."[43]

Supporting the idea that gossip plays a role in moral education, empirical studies show that gossipers do not just talk about anything. They are particularly attracted to subject matters with high moral content. In fact, gossipers are often found to talk about moral taboos. (That people gossip about sexual infidelity is not just a cliché!) In a dissertation project entitled, "Gossip as a vehicle for value comparison: The development of social norms and social bonding through moral judgment," social psychologist Holly Doy Wah Hom found that a full 41 percent of her respondents gave only two examples of prototypical gossip: they told a story either about sexual activity or about infidelity.[44] Drinking, dating, and provocative behavior each made it into at least 10 percent of the stories Young collected.[45] Apparently gossipers do use gossip as a means of discussing morally loaded subjects.

Gossip has also been shown to impart moral lessons, as we heard Lischer, Norris, and Willimon suggest. Social scientists have long suspected that gossip facilitates "cultural learning" through the sharing of information and anecdotes. In one recent study, psychologists propose that "gossip comes in handy" because it is "a potentially powerful and efficient means of transmitting information about the rules, norms, and other guidelines for living in a culture."[46] They asked fifty-eight undergraduate students in an introductory psychology class to describe a piece of gossip they had recently heard and to answer various questions about the incident, including whether they had learned anything from the gossip. Sixty-four percent confirmed that the gossip they heard had, in fact, taught them something. The authors argued that if recipients benefited from hearing gossip, this suggests that gossip is neither merely idle talk nor simply a vehicle for the gossiper to vent aggressive feelings. Thus, gossip was rehabilitated, in their eyes, as a teacher of cultural norms. "Gossip can be understood as an extension of observational learning, in the sense that people can learn about the complexities of social and cultural life by hearing about the successes and especially misadventures of others."[47] In other words, gossip is indeed like learning a lesson vicariously, which is less risky than having to learn it "the hard way."

And yet one can still doubt whether the lessons learned through gossip genuinely lead to greater interpersonal trust. Do we find trust being built among gossipers because one person dispenses moral advice to another who risks admitting that she needs it? Perhaps. But if this were the case, then we would expect the advice to be tailored to the gossip recipient's concern. We would expect, furthermore, that the lessons imparted would be thoughtful and fresh, testing rather than accepting the standard advice. In point of fact, when one listens to a lot of gossip, as researchers do, one tends to hear very little that is truly novel and most of it instead a recycling of old clichés. When one examines how the undergraduates in the above-mentioned study answered the question of what they learned from gossip, for example, the answers seem remarkably prosaic: "'Just don't drink'; 'Don't forget your true friends'; 'Infidelity will eventually catch up with you' . . . 'People usually find out what you try to hide'; 'Long distance relationships are difficult to manage,' and so forth. In fact, the research team admitted that "Most of their answers took the form of generalizations that would be useful maxims for their own social life."[48] Combined with the overwhelming evidence that people tend only to gossip with those they already know well—a consensus in the literature—it seems that while gossip may sometimes serve an educative function, it usually comes in the form of a reminder about something the receiver ought to know anyway. Thus, it does not appear to break new moral ground that the recipient needs broken.

If gossip served an educative role in ways that facilitated trust, one would expect that it would get easier for gossips and gossip recipients to hear and express hard truths. Gossip would eventually open people up to face life's difficult lessons. But in the chapter of her book immediately following "The Holy Use of Gossip," Kathleen Norris effectively admits that gossip does not encourage people to build relationships of candor and honesty. Asking and answering the question, "Can You Tell the Truth in a Small Town?" she concludes that no, for the most part, you cannot. You cannot really tell the truth in a small town because the close-knit and insular nature of small towns actually renders the truth too raw, not, as one might imagine, easier to accept. The "truths" she addresses are specific to the geographical region that is her topic: in the Dakotas, too many farms have failed, too many sons and daughters have fled, too many families have gone bankrupt. Many small towns are dying and have been for some time, and thus they carry a collective hurt produced by the nostalgia of once-better days. The point is that small towns are not the secure, supportive places everyone believes them to be. Local history is frequently rewritten, erasing the "discouraging word" from home on the range.[49] The truth is otherwise too painful and too close. Norris goes on to confess that small-town inhabitants not only rewrite their history but their present as well. "A more immediate consequence of the local history mentality is the tendency to 'make nice.' If we can make the past harmonious, why not the present? Why risk discussion that might cause unpleasantness?"[50] She recalls an instance when the committee searching for a new pastor at her church tried to avoid a candid conversation about how young of a candidate they could hope to attract. The reality of the increasing average age of pastors, she said, merely reminded them of how rapidly their own congregation was graying. One woman tried to curtail the conversation by protesting that their wish for a young pastor wasn't really serious: "Oh, we didn't mean anything. It was all in fun."[51]

If even our open, structured conversations have a tendency to get whitewashed, why should we expect gossip to be any more salutary? Gossip may not be idle, but it is hardly a rigorous form of talk. We should not expect people to challenge themselves with new ideas, reverse their biases, or confront their doubts and fears when they gossip. In short, we should not expect gossipers to take great risks. *Gossip is not about risk taking.* Its content is very often trite and the morals of its stories standard fare. If anything, gossip tends to be about avoiding confrontation and skirting potentially difficult truths. It tends to repel genuine risk.

In fact, evidence suggests that the main risk gossipers face is when they try to stop it. Among those who study adolescence, there is a frequently cited 1991 study of the gossip behavior of eighth-grade girls. It showed that gossip followed a well-worn groove. "It typically began with an explicitly evaluative statement, and unless this statement was immediately challenged, others present were likely to concur with and elaborate on the negative evaluation."[52] One example will suffice to demonstrate the spiral:

> *Penny:* In choir, that girl was sitting in front of us and we kept going, 'Moo.'

Karen: We were going, 'Come here cow. Come here cow.'

Penny: And that girl kept going.

Bonnie: I know. She is one.

Penny: She looks like a big fat cow.

Julie: Who is that?

Bonnie: That girl on the basketball team.

Penny: That big redheaded cow.

Bonnie: From Clintonville.

Julie: Oh, yeah. I know. She is a cow.[53]

In other words, it was very difficult to redirect the flow of a conversation once started. If a girl disagreed with the gossip producer's initial remark, she had to voice her disagreement immediately. Otherwise, she was ignored. Those conducting the study found that departures from or counters to the original evaluative statement were rare after the first exchange. Instead, as noted, most girls went along with the first opinion expressed. Counteropinions expressed right away, however, might be entertained. The upshot of this study is that girls can take seriously the opinions expressed in gossip and challenge them, but to do so they have to act swiftly. In effect, they have to interrupt the otherwise predictable flow of gossip. Since interrupting one's friends to disagree with them is known to be difficult for many young teenage girls, attempts to stop or correct gossip can be considered a significant social risk on their part. In all likelihood, it is not only adolescent girls who find that the riskiest part of gossip is ending it.[54]

Vulnerability

We have already begun to sense the relationship between gossip and vulnerability. Gossip is a practice that makes those being talked about vulnerable to those doing the talking. This does not mean that targets are always hurt by gossip because gossip *can* flatter them. Moreover, some people acknowledge that they are vulnerable to the gossip grapevine but prefer being in that situation to being ignored. As one person put it, "At least I know that when people talk about me, they consider me 'in'." Being a target of gossip, then, though a vulnerable position to be in, is not necessarily without its merits.

Still other people claim that they participate in gossip to ease their feelings of vulnerability vis-à-vis some social group into which they are trying to fit. Gossip has, in fact, been shown to help people avoid embarrassment and anxiety by "teaching" them how to behave appropriately. By this we do not necessarily mean moral behavior, as discussed above, but behavior appropriate to the situation. As one team of social psychologists concluded:

> By listening to peers gossip, one can learn valuable lessons about how to behave or, more commonly perhaps, how *not* to behave. One learns how others in the peer group might have discussed one's behavior had one not conformed to social expectations. Indeed, parables related during gossip—third-hand lessons about what can happen if one commits a certain behavior—are powerful teachers of social skills and social norms.[55]

Because gossip is by definition about someone *else*, one can avoid being confronted directly about one's own behavior. One can avoid potential *faux pas* without having to admit ignorance.

Participating in gossip can also ease the anxiety that comes with being new or uninformed. In fact, this function of gossip has even been given a nickname: the "freshman class" gossip phenomenon. Empirically, it has been shown that incoming members of a community (for instance, the freshman class of a school) gossip more actively than senior members. One study of residential assistants (RAs) in a college dormitory system showed that RAs who were new to the role tended to seek out gossip more often than did seasoned ones. This study employed a technique called social network analysis and found that RAs fell into distinct categories in terms of their gossip behavior: RAs with the longest tenure gossiped with a lot of different people, but overall reported gossiping less frequently and not always or even mostly concerning RA advice. Newer RAs, in contrast, gossiped both widely and frequently, and much of their gossip had to do with being an RA. The author summarizes the difference by saying that "the second group was *getting* in touch with the network; the first group was *staying* in touch."[56] His findings support the idea that one's gossip activity declines upon feeling more comfortable in one's social setting, or, to put it conversely, that gossip can help ease social vulnerability.

A simple anecdote illustrates how gossip can ameliorate vulnerability in all the ways we have just discussed: by teaching behavioral lessons, stemming anxiety, and letting one fit in socially:

> A specific example comes from a friend who recalled her first couple of years as a high school teacher. They were ridden with malicious gossip.

She remembers teachers talking badly about one another, and she remembers taking comfort from these discussions. Maybe she was not as bad a teacher as she had feared; there were worse teachers, according to the gossip. She remembers feeling compelled to gossip negatively with other teachers to feel a part of the group, to feel better about her own skills in relation to other 'freshman' teachers, and to learn what *not* to do as a teacher. Now in her fourth year, and at a new school, she avoids gossiping at work. The reason, she believes, is that she is now confident in her abilities as a teacher and is less concerned with what others think. In other words, she avoids negative gossip at work because she does not need it as much. No longer is she in a situation in which she feels uncertain, anxious, and without friends.[57]

And so we might conclude that gossip facilitates trust by helping people feel less vulnerable in new settings. Is it not equally possible to conclude, however, that because their gossip behavior wanes with time, trust takes away the need for people to gossip? Trust, as we have previously imagined it, invites people into greater and greater risks, leading to greater and greater trust. But if the practice of gossip follows a "freshman class" pattern, this suggests that gossip may be unlike trust. People may cease needing to gossip but they never cease needing to trust.

Power

Finally, we have argued that trust and power exist in creative tension with one another. People with less power have to trust those with more, but when bestowed wisely, their trust can work to mitigate the more pernicious exercises of power. Being entrusted with something valuable, in other words, both increases and humanizes one's power. Does gossip work the same way?

Perhaps some of the most compelling research on gossip and its relationship to power comes from the corner of the psychology world interested in the development of girls and young women. Developmental psychologists look not only at gossip, of course, but at a range of behaviors that change as girls mature into adolescence. At the risk of reinforcing the centuries-old stereotype that gossip is a female activity, they confirm that gossip plays a special role in the lives of girls and young women. Unfortunately, this role is ambivalent at best: gossip provides some relief from the pressures of girlhood but can also be transformed into psychological warfare. The latter use of gossip is apparently so common, in fact, that it has caught the attention of feminist scholars interested in understanding the causes of female childhood aggression, or girl bullying.

In *Girlfighting: Betrayal and Rejection Among Girls*, Lyn Mikel Brown argues that as girls grow up, they find themselves increasingly trapped in a peculiar struggle between expressing all their emotions, including anger, and at the same time desiring to remain the polite, well-behaved girls they have been taught to be. If a girl has always been cautioned against being "mean" (and, to summarize a wealth of literature in one declaration, girls *are* cautioned against this more than boys), then how does she express anger? Feminists have persuasively demonstrated that the familial and cultural pressures placed on girls to be "sugar and spice and everything nice" can become overwhelming. It is natural for children occasionally to feel rage and want to fight with their peers. And yet girls in particular receive harsher social reprimands for aggressive demonstrations of power. For whatever reason, boys' fighting is better tolerated. Fighting seems somehow contradictory to being a girl. This contradiction causes a psychic split, Brown argues, within a girl who feels nasty but wants to appear nice. "Part of being an acceptable girl in a culture so deeply infused with white middle-class values, is to be, or at least appear to be, 'nice.' So girls who buy into prevailing views of femininity are likely to hide the 'bad' or 'shameful' parts of their relationships when they can."[58] Thus, girls often try to remain "nice" at all costs, even if it means seeking other ways of expressing their feelings. These other ways include what Brown calls "girlfighting," which includes such behaviors as spreading rumors, shunning, and bad-mouthing.

And gossip. Gossip is one strategy, as we have seen, for expressing feelings without really expressing them, by commenting on someone *else's* life. Gossip thus becomes an important weapon in girls' arsenal. It is "one way to deal with frustration and anger too risky to express directly."[59] As they seek desperately to solve the riddle of appearing nice on the outside while staying true to themselves on the inside, they say mean things about other girls but in a flippant, gossipy way. Being gossip, their mean statements cannot be traced with certainty back to them, and they can always deny them if challenged. Thus, girls achieve the feat of keeping their reputation as a "nice girl" while simultaneously venting at least some of their negative thoughts and feelings. It is a way, however perverse, to regain some of the power denied them by oppressive gender expectations. "Girlfighting is not a biological necessity, a developmental stage, or rite of passage. It is a protective strategy and an avenue to power learned and nurtured in early childhood and perfected over time."[60]

But since gossip is almost always contained to one's social circle, why do girls need to target their own friends in order to give voice to their anger? Girls are not, after all, always only angry at their close friends. Brown confirms the irony. Girls not only demonstrate through their actions, but also confirm verbally, their reliance on other girls to satisfy a need for close personal friendship. And yet they appear to turn on those same friends quite often. Brown and other feminists explain this kind of betrayal as a response to a sexist culture in which girls are pressured to seek approval, especially from men. It is not enough for them simply to be who they are and call that good. If they are unsuccessful in receiving enough favorable recognition naturally, they are forced to secure it for themselves by explicitly comparing themselves approvingly to their cohorts.[61] Gossip, in other words, can increase their sense of power in a context of powerlessness. Brown calls this "jealously protecting one's small piece of patriarchal pie from other women."[62] The point, again, is that gossip is used in an attempt to empower the self. Unfortunately, of course, it seizes power at the expense of the other.

At its worst, gossip becomes a tool of what scholars call "relational aggression." Relational aggression is the expression of nonphysical violence or force, especially by the less powerful individuals in a social group. Often associated with girls rather than boys, it means hurting another person by harming her social relationships. Relational aggression is expressed through a range of nonphysical behaviors. Clinical psychologist Marion Underwood describes it this way:

> When girls feel angry or resentful, they hurt one another sometimes by fighting physically, but more often by verbal insults, friendship manipulation, or nonverbal expressions of disgust or disdain. . . . Girls hurt each other's feelings by social exclusion via sneers, verbal comments, nasty notes, *gossip*, and electronic mail.[63]

Underwood's research confirms that relational aggression can be found among girls as young as three years old. Harming someone else's relationships is a covert and indirect way to hurt them, as explained above. Gossip, with its subversive, underground nature, is the perfect tactic for girls who have acquired verbal competency. In some communities, girls' aggressive gossip has become so bad that parents have sought to intervene. Some parents have transferred their daughters out of one school into another simply to remove them from the devastating effects of gossip. Other parents teach their daughters how to fight back. Parent groups have begun to insist that gossip be recognized as a form of bullying and addressed in antibullying programs in the local schools. Brown notes:

> After an elementary school was praised in our local paper for the success of its . . . antibullying program, a man wrote a letter expressing his outrage. His niece, he said, never benefitted from the curriculum.
>
> She is constantly picked on and ostracized at that school—my heart breaks for her whenever she tells me about the other girls in her class and the cruel way they treat her. Recently, one girl invited all the kids in her class—except my niece—to her birthday party.[64]

Certainly gossip does not always get this nasty. My point in showing it at its worst is to underline the relationship between gossip and power. In the wrong hands (mouths), gossip can become a powerful social force for hurting others. As literary theorist Spacks puts it, "If other people handle my secrets, discuss my character, describe me as worse than I hope I am, they threaten my integrity."[65] And yet, ironically, gossip is often used precisely by those with less social power. It is no accident that gossip has been associated throughout time with women rather than men. Gossip, as we have seen, constitutes a covert, indirect use of power. It therefore thrives among those who cannot afford direct shows of power but who nevertheless need somehow to counter the use of power against them.

Thus, Spacks argues that among women, gossip represents a subversive resistance to sexist power. She relates a story about gossip that has a long history in folklore. It is the tale of the husband who shares with his wife the secret that he has laid two eggs. Unable to contain her incredulity, she repeats to her women friends what her husband has told her. Her "gossip" gets back to her husband. Enraged, he drags her before the community and publicly shames her. As Spacks notes, the traditional rendering of this story is as cautionary tale: Do not spill the secrets your spouse shares with you. A nontraditional, feminist reading is very different: a woman has every right to turn to her community in the face of a husband who has not only the power to get away with claiming to have achieved a highly dubious feat (and a female one at that, laying eggs) but also the power to humiliate her in public. "She needs such community in order to resist an imposition of power."[66]

Women, of course, are not the only powerless social group. If we return to our original understanding of gossip as one way of seeking information about others when information is scarce, we would expect any group to gossip that feels undeservedly cut off from information. It should be no wonder that clerical workers, middle managers, associates to rectors, and others low on the totem pole of institutional power are notorious gossipers. They are frequently the ones excluded from sources of information and from decision making. When producers of knowledge hoard that knowledge, there will inevitably be those who try to penetrate its barrier. As one defender of gossip puts it: "Those who remain shut off from the bastions of commonly recognized social and political power will continue to look to gossip as one form of inquiry, knowing, and power available to them as other forms are not."[67]

Thus, our moral evaluation of gossip cannot be a simply straightforward condemnation of it. We must understand who uses gossip and why. We must admit that gossip satisfies needs for power that often go unrecognized and unmet. That it comes out as a way to satisfy unattractive emotions like rage, envy, and jealousy should not blind us to its subversive benefits, mixed as those might be. As for gossip and trust, we cannot simply counsel people to stop gossiping and trust each other instead, for "trust" in the context of an unequal power balance is not the kind of trust we want.

DOES GOSSIP SERVE TRUST?

Empirical studies by no means give us a definitive picture of gossip, let alone a way to evaluate it as a practice of faith. And yet the studies cited here, taken together, support a picture with which I believe many of us would agree: gossip is at best voyeuristic, at worst, hurtfully invasive. Certainly I would agree that there is a time and place in our lives for leisurely, nonserious banter. I would agree with those who point out its social utility. And, as just noted, gossip sometimes reflects a desperate plea for power more than anything else. But none of these reasons for gossip make it a form of expression worth aspiring to. In none of the studies I consulted did I hear an unmitigated positive assessment of gossip. All the different defenses of gossip are just that—defenses. None of its apologists wish to come out and say that gossip is a salutary thing. At best they say that gossip seems to be a universal human activity (and thus we had better get used to it) and typically not all that harmful. Even Aaron Ben-Ze´ev was forced to conclude his essay entitled "The Vindication of Gossip" with a statement that hardly vindicated it: "Gossip is not a virtuous activity; I have tried to show that it is not vicious either."[68]

But only virtuous practices will foster trust. Gossip has inherent problems that militate against its ability to build genuine trust. Let us briefly look at it again from the perspective of the target, the individual being talked about. Even in its mildest versions, gossip thrives at that person's expense. The expense may not be great, and some might even wonder whether we can always discern an effect on those being discussed— precisely because they are *not* privy to the discussion. But talking about someone without their knowledge is harmful if only because they deserve to know. If gossip satisfies our curiosity about other people's lives, and even if this curiosity is fairly benign, it still remains the case that *our* curiosity gets satisfied at the expense of *their* curiosity about what we are thinking and saying! At the very least, targets of gossip experience what those excluded from secrets experience: being cut off from knowledge concerning them.

Beyond this, targets may bear the expense of gossip in any of the following ways: by becoming the butt of jokes, the open book, the cautionary tale, the standard against which the gossipers measure their own lives, the lightning rod for community debate, the handy example for those who like to moralize. When speech becomes gossip, the subject is no longer the reality of another person's life, but a convenient version of it. Information about people becomes no longer just information but amusement, entertainment, a lesson. When targets become the butts of jokes, the cautionary tales, and so forth, they become depersonalized. They are made into versions of themselves, available for others' perusal and discussion. As even the very term *target* itself suggests, the person being talked about is figuratively as well as literally distanced from the talkers. She or he is set at a remove, for the others' convenience. As target, she becomes someone other than her true self. Her full humanity is flattened, and she becomes an object for others to appreciate as they assess her through the crosshairs.

The gossipers' distance from their target also significantly reduces their accountability for what they say. Gossip succeeds as a "practice" because specific statements cannot be traced back to the practitioners. Gossip is about looseness, freedom, lack of inhibition. People gossip because they can. In other words, gossip lets them escape not only the burden of accuracy but also the burden of authorship. I can say something without having it be remanded to me. I can half-claim it. I can be a pseudo-authority on the topic. Gossip is a form of speech, like the increasingly popular Internet "blog," that exists at a remove from actual interpersonal encounters. It relies on anonymity. It is "virtual" information sharing, with all the moral ambiguity that accompanies "virtual" human experiences. One can argue that anonymity supports freedom of speech: one can test out new and potentially scandalous ideas, take a stand on unpopular views, even soften the blow of damning opinion. And yet, in the end, gossip, like other forms of unauthorized authority, inevitably sacrifices genuine human engagement for mere human expression.

As such, gossip is ultimately a form of social avoidance. Like "talking" to our buddies via an Internet blog and thus avoiding the potential awkwardness of actually meeting them, talking to our circle of fellow gossipers lets us spin attractive anecdotes, express uncritical opinions, and offer half-baked advice rather than do the hard work of figuring out the lives of other human beings and what we really think about them. It lets us encounter people within a limited context rather than in the fullness of their being.

Moreover, gossip is a kind of discourse that achieves its function without appearing to have any function. In fact, it succeeds *because* it seems to lack any function. Gossip is a purposeful form of speech that masquerades as purposeless. (Gossipers themselves love to call their talk "idle.") It *has* to be purposeless, or else it would be utterly condemned and cease to function. Gossip thrives as a social practice only because people do not look too hard at its practice. Gossip trades on its supposed levity. Our moral blitheness about gossip is like gossip itself: killed when it gets too serious.

Patricia Meyer Spacks suggests that our ambivalence about gossip is connected to our ambivalent attitudes toward language more generally. On the one hand, we know that words matter. "The idea of talking in secret—i.e., without the subject's knowledge—about someone recalls old conceptions of words as dangerous weapons."[69] On the other hand, we tend to deny that the words we utter actually make any difference. We have difficulty—or we claim to—with thinking of anything we simply *say*, and do not act on, as having genuinely destructive potential. The classic childhood chant, "Sticks and stones can break my bones, but words will never hurt me," perfectly demonstrates our ambivalence. It acknowledges the power we ascribe to language while simultaneously attempting to subdue it.[70] Gossip thus endures in part because of our ambivalent beliefs about language. Due to the blurry moral assessment we make of language's harm in general, we have a difficult time condemning gossip morally.

In conclusion, gossip is rife with internal contradictions. Bergmann calls it a "discreet indiscretion." The paradox is important. If gossip were not discreet—that is, if gossip producers did not choose carefully their recipients and disburse their tidbits of information selectively, but rather just broadcasted their information indiscriminately—then gossip would die as a practice. But if it were not an indiscretion, then it would likewise die. The social intimacy between producer and recipient that is the point of gossip rests on the mutually guilty pleasure they share. Bergmann believes that if today's rehabilitators of gossip (like our pastoral theologians) have their way in removing its guilty taint, they will actually ruin the fun of gossip and thus gossip itself.

With our own interest in trust in mind, we have seen that gossip does the opposite of helping people take wise risks, accept appropriate vulnerability, and balance power inequalities. In fact, it undermines all these attempts. The practice of gossip encourages people to ignore the riskiness of language, downplay the vulnerability of social status, reinforce hegemonic ideas, and let stand imbalances of power. Is there a practice of sharing information that can substitute?

TESTIMONY

Chris's speech in the third vignette with which we began this chapter is an example of gossip's alternative. We conclude this chapter by comparing gossip to another practice, that of public testimony. I am not trying to suggest that testimony will satisfy gossipers, but I will argue that testimony bears many similarities to gossip and is preferable from a moral point of view.

Testimony, as I define it, is first-person, public revelation of oneself and one's faith. Testimonials witness to some truth about life with God in the community of faith. In the context of worship, they usually take the form of oral storytelling or praise giving whereby one person stands in front of the rest and speaks about their faith. Testimony is, as Thomas Hoyt Jr. writes in *Practicing Our Faith*, "a deeply shared practice—one that is possible only in a community that recognizes that falsehood is strong, but that yearns nonetheless to know what is true and good."[71] Testimony satisfies people's curiosity about others in their community while strengthening social bonds, offering constructive lessons, and building the faith— all without the need to talk behind another's back. We could say that testimony is gossip gone public. It shares many of the features of gossip but is practiced within public rather than private relationships. Testimony is a communal, or public, practice because "although only one person may be speaking at a time, that person's speech takes place within the context of other people's listening, expecting, and encouraging."[72]

This initial description may make testimony sound like an entirely different practice from gossip, but interestingly, the two share some important features. Historically, the practice of testimony arose among oppressed peoples who needed a covert way to share expressions of their pain and anger. African American slaves testified to the goodness of God's deliverance of them as expressed in biblical stories but the testimony also referred to the conditions they yearned to be delivered *from*. If their captors heard these testimonies, however, they would miss the slaves' subversive references to their captivity and their hope for freedom and would simply hear God being praised. Thus, testimony became a powerful tool of expression that still resonates in African American worship today, especially in communities where social and political power is still an only partially realized dream. It can be a way for people of all backgrounds to claim the power denied them by their social reality.

Faith communities of many colors and stripes have rediscovered the value of testimony as a theological practice in corporate worship and beyond. Individuals not unlike Chris get up and offer publicly their hope for what is "true and good" in their lives. The practice can have transformative effects upon a congregation, and it strikes me that the effects are related to the fact that through testimony people are invited to take risk, accept vulnerability, and share power.

Testimony, especially for those who are new to it, represents public risk taking. Lillian Daniel has written about introducing a practice of testimony into a local (mostly middle-class, New England) congregation.[73] She attests to the risk: "It takes a lot of nerve to share our faith publicly and requires some people to stretch themselves almost to the limit."[74] People have to stretch themselves not just because testimony is a form of public speaking (nearly universally feared) but because it is a public form of personal sharing. And yet testimony is a chosen and calculated risk. It is vastly different from being the *target* of other people's words. With testimony, one intentionally authors one's own ideas and deliberately shares them with everyone in the community. Ultimately, this transforms the experience of risk into one of safety.

With testimony, the risk is not necessarily the individual's alone. Even when a testimony is "vetted" by the pastor or worship leader, the congregation usually does not know what they are about to hear. Spontaneous testimony opens the community up to expressions of both pain and hope that they cannot anticipate and sometimes cannot handle adequately. When the pastor refrains from editing the testimonies to be offered, she relinquishes control she might otherwise exercise in worship over theological and political content. In other words, the whole church takes a risk in hearing each other's testimonies. Daniel admitted:

> But what if someone were to stand up and offer a cruel or crazy vision? What if someone were to use the moment to bring forth a grudge or an agenda that reflected poorly on the church? . . . It takes a confident church to introduce testimony, I suspect, one that is willing to face the unpredictable and to release some control. But it is in the very release of control that the blessings come.[75]

Part of the beauty of testimony is letting laypeople give voice to truths that ordained leaders might never express, and there are other blessings testimony awakens that often balance its risks.

Testimony can produce vulnerability. It is not an easy thing to be listened to intently by others who you know are taking you seriously.

> Even though testifiers were delighted with the warm response they received, we are still human and cannot help but judge ourselves. We imagine that our words pale in comparison to those offered by another person, and even when testifying to God's grace, we still suffer under the need to do a good job. The Holy Spirit may be at work, but it does not take away everybody's anxiety all the time.[76]

Therefore, Daniel urges those communities who would begin to practice testimony to learn to practice *hospitality* first. "It strikes me that in order to encourage testimony, you must first practice hospitality, so that speakers will have the sense that the words they entrust to the community will be valued and not denigrated."[77] In the terms of this book, testimonies must be offered in safe spaces so that the risk taken will be commensurate to the relationship, and the vulnerability kept appropriate.

I see not only an analogy but also a potential connection between the practices of testimony and gossip. I suspect that letting members of the community speak directly to one another might obviate their need to gossip. In testimony, they talk about the very same things they would gossip about, after all—their upbringing, their personal failures, their temptations, and their successes. Testimonies can be quite candid. In my experience, they often broadcast the very juicy details people are curious about! Moreover, testimony bonds people together in unexpected ways, both small and great. Mention the state from which one hails, and one is certain to be greeted during coffee hour by everyone else who grew up there. Confess one's struggles with depression, and one will engender many quiet, knowing gestures of support. Testimony draws people together in the same casual ways lauded so fervently by those who defend gossip, without the voyeurism. It proves that formal modes of speech *can* have the same effects as informal talk.

Finally, the practice of testimony empowers people. People experience a sense of elation and power once they have given their testimonies. Laypeople who express in their testimony a political or theological stance different from that of the pastor feel that they have been able to satisfy their need for a voice, and for keeping diversity of opinion alive. Testimony may even offer a public and constructive way for disagreements to be aired and thus welcomed.[78] Energy gets produced by this exciting and (for some of us) novel form of speech. Publicly testifying to one's Christian faith is a very powerful thing. It transforms people. "It is a practice that feels risky, but rewards richly."[79]

In conclusion, when gossip in the church goes public, it becomes testimony. It retains its power as a form of discourse but loses many of its moral faults. Risk, vulnerability, and power are transformed from dangers into blessings. This is what it means to trust.

Chapter Five

ꙮ BULLSHIT

Any practice can be practiced well or poorly. The last chapter promoted testimony as an alternative practice to gossip, arguing that while gossip has a tendency to undermine trust, testimony can nurture it. Generally speaking, this is true. It must be acknowledged, however, that even testimony can be done badly. Not everyone given the chance to express themselves in the pulpit or lectern will sparkle with wit or inspiration. Some will ramble on too long, strain for the right tone, exaggerate their piety. Some testifiers will annoy or bore or even anger their audience. Few of them will risk telling the whole truth about their lives, especially when it comes to their faith. Some can end up, in effect, gossiping about their spiritual lives, rather than attempting the more difficult feat of talking about something they know to be true and real. Testifiers with an axe to grind or a grudge to bear can strain the experience for their listeners, as can those with unorthodox theological views. When it comes to announcing the good news, in short, the Holy Spirit does not always find the perfect mouthpiece. At its worst, the danger of letting people speak in the name of the Lord is that they will betray the faith we entrusted in them when we agreed to listen.

In her short story entitled "Personal Testimony," Lynna Williams gives a name to the particular failure of humans to praise the Lord in speech. "Jesus Jaw," she calls it, "a malady that makes it impossible for the devoted to say what they mean and sit down."[1] In the story, the term is coined in reference to the endlessly awful revival meetings her protagonist has to endure at a Southern Baptist summer camp in Oklahoma, but we have probably all encountered church people afflicted with this malady. In part, they simply cannot find the right words to express their faith, for finding words can indeed be difficult. As Bobby Dunn, Williams's character who suffers from "Jesus Jaw" puts it, "I know what I want to say, but it comes out all wrong." But mostly the malady seems to stem from a combination of self-righteousness and cowardice—the fear that saying anything less than profound will mark one as un-Christian. Those with a bad case of Jesus Jaw are often the most desperate to appear more certain or more devout than they really are. In their ambition to honor Jesus, perhaps even to be Jesus-like, the *effect* of their words takes precedence over veracity. I call this pastoral bullshit, and I argue that we hear it more often from the mouths of clergy than from ordinary believers. Bullshitters care less about being honest and more about impressing or placating their audience and the result is a sort of spiritual nonsense. This offends the listener who expected something more honest when they agreed to listen, and thus bullshit is a moral problem in the church. It is a variant of lying and a violation of trust. The ethics of bullshit will occupy us for most of the chapter, but before we get too far ahead of ourselves, let us return to Williams's story.

Williams's protagonist, a Southern Baptist girl of twelve and daughter of a preacher, sets herself up in business at "Faith Camp" writing other campers' testimonies. During swim period, she sneaks to a corner of the arts-and-crafts cabin, where she meets her fellow campers and listens to their tales of spiritual angst. Back in her bunk at night, with a flashlight under the covers, she composes their testimony. She delivers the final product to them by 5:00 P.M. the next day, thus providing her campmates with something eloquent to say if called upon during the evening tent meeting. It is Bobby Dunn's "Jesus Jaw" that starts it. He sees no problem with engaging someone else's services in producing the testimony he would give in worship; he calls it "a sort of ghostwriting service for Jesus."[2]

For her part, the business lets her exercise her twin evil passions—profiting from other campers' incompetence with language while simultaneously mocking the very practice of Christian testimony. Her hypocrisy is all the more scandalous since her father is the pastor and would be mortified to learn that his own daughter is authoring other people's testimonies at Faith Camp. This, however, turns out to be central to the appeal. She desperately wants to settle a moral score with her father. She has begun this business, we learn, to seek revenge for her father's own hypocrisy toward her: three years earlier, her father had told her she was adopted and swore her to secrecy regarding her identity.

Even though I assure my customers with every sale that we will never get caught, I never write a testimony without imagining public exposure of my wrongdoing. The scene is so familiar to me that I do not have to close my eyes to see it: the summons to the camp director's office and the door closing behind me; the shocked faces of the other campers when the news leaks out; the Baptist Academy girls who comb their hair and go in pairs, bravely, to offer my brother comfort; the automatic rotation of my name to the top of everyone's prayer list. I spend hours imagining the small details of my shame, always leading to the moment when my father, called from Fort Worth to take me home, arrives at camp.

That will be my moment. I have done something so terrible that even my father will not be able to keep it a secret. I am doing this because of my father's secrets.[3]

As events unfold, she is nearly denied her moment of glory. It is the last night of camp, and the worship service has reached the point where campers will offer testimonies, and then her father, just in from Fort Worth, will preach. When the director issues the call for testimonies and one of the boys gets up to deliver one of her masterpieces, her father intercepts him and starts toward the pulpit himself. Taken completely aback, she looks at her father closely, and realizes from his demeanor and behavior that he knows about the testimony business, and that he is about to take matters into his own hands by stepping forward and forgiving her. To her, this would be the worst possible thing to happen, and she cannot let him do it. From her seat in the choir loft, she sprints to the pulpit. Beating him there, she immediately launches into testimony.

I begin by admitting what I have been doing for the past three weeks. I talk about being gripped by hate, unable to appreciate the love of my wonderful parents or of Jesus. I talk about making money from other campers who, in their honest desire to honor the Lord, become trapped in my web of wrongdoing. . . .

For an instant I lose control and begin quoting poetry instead of Scripture. There is a shaky moment when all I can remember is bits of "Stopping by Woods on a Snowy Evening," but I manage to tie the verses back to a point about Christian choices. The puzzled looks on some faces give way to shouts of "Amen!" and as I look out at the rows of people in the green-and-white-striped tent I know I have won. I have written the best testimony anyone at camp has ever given.[4]

Williams's story raises interesting questions about the ethics of testimony. It contrasts the morally dubious strategy of hiring a ghostwriter, undertaken by those afflicted with "Jesus Jaw" who know that their practice of testimony suffers, with the equally dubious strategy of lying in a testimony about your true frame of mind. (Hers is a common enough strategy that it even has a nickname: "testilying.") Surely we cannot agree with the protagonist that her testimony is the "best testimony" ever, laden as we know it to be with ulterior motives and false piety. And yet perhaps we can agree that it is in at least one sense better than the works of art she has forged for other campers, for it comes directly from the heart of the one speaking. So we are left wondering: What *does* constitute the "best testimony"? Or, rather, since we might not especially wish to praise any of the testimonies in the story: Which testimonies were worse, morally speaking? The ones our protagonist penned for others, or the one she delivered herself?

One might initially want to argue for the latter. Surely it is worse to pretend you are remorseful than it is to get someone else to put a few words together for you. Being "gripped by hate" and unable to appreciate the love of others are not the real motivations for the girl's actions, so her testimony is in effect a false confession. She accepts accountability for her actions but does not really tell the truth about them. Her real desires are to "win" the audience that night and to embarrass her father, and she accomplishes both. This testimony puts one in mind of the autobiographies and memoirs one reads that are filled with unflattering content about other people.[5] As a reader, one begins to question whether the shaming of others is as much a motivation for the autobiographer than anything else.[6] One starts to lose sympathy and make the kind of judgments one has suspended for the sake of what one literary critic has called the autobiographical "pact" between reader and writer (not unlike the trust relationship as we have defined it).[7] Another kind of autobiographical betrayal occurs when the writer's account is later revealed to contain events that could not or did not really happen.[8] A testifier's credibility in church is as important as an author's is in print and just as damaging to others when destroyed.

Nevertheless, despite all these valid reasons for judging the final testimony the worst rather than the best one of the summer (morally speaking), I find myself rooting for the girl as the heroine of the summer and of this story. In fact I find myself decidedly unimpressed by the moral character of her campmates. I am bothered more by their parade all summer of inauthentic recitations being offered in the name of testimony than by her impulsive, if less than honest, witness. Why? What might make sense of my response?

First of all, the story shows that she worked quite hard on behalf of her customers to represent them accurately (whether or not they shared this concern). She spends time with them, conducting research into the particulars of what sin each of them has to confess. The testimonies she crafts are received and believed by their audience because they are based on something real. They show her to be committed to a certain kind of honesty even while undertaking an enterprise she knows to be wrong. Second, and more important, her little cottage industry is made possible in the first place only because others are too ineffectual or too self-protective to speak their own words. Bobby Dunn, "blond, ambitious, and in love with Jesus, is Faith Camp's standard for male perfection,"[9] and yet *he* is the one to approach *her* with the idea. (His hypocrisy is underscored when he then looks down on her decision to charge money.) Who is in the wrong here? The actual author of the words, putting pen to paper for the sake of more beautiful speech, or the buyer of words, too proud to risk expressing himself if it might come out sounding awkward?

For me, Williams's story testifies to the power of authorship and to the moral preference for speakers themselves embodying the words they speak.[10] The reason testimony is better than gossip, I argued, is that with testimony the subject is also the author/ity. Having someone else author your own testimony is wrong for the same reason. It is like plagiarism. You no longer yourself say what you mean. It is cowardly and cheap. We saw in the last chapter, moreover, how empowering it can be to stand up and tell the story of your life and faith. To make this point more fully, however, I must explain the way the story ends, for the protagonist's testimony does not constitute the conclusion.

What happens next, in fact, makes the reader think at first that her victory in the pulpit will be voided. After the final hymn has been sung, and all the worshipers including Bobby Dunn have hugged her and forgiven her, she is alone with her father. He speaks no words, but, rather, reaches up and slaps her hard on the face, even drawing blood where his ring hits her cheekbone. Nevertheless, through her tears she sees that he is crying. The story closes with her extending an arm to him in a gesture of reconciliation.

Why does Williams make the girl the first one to forgive? Why, for that matter, had the girl refused her father's forgiveness all along? Why had she dreamed all summer instead of the moment when her when her shameful deeds will become public? The answers to these questions lie, I believe, in the power of authoring one's own story, both figuratively and literally.

The girl knows that power is conferred upon the one who speaks, and the one who is made to keep silent remains powerless. When, on her ninth birthday, her father reveals to her the secret of her adoption, she does not need to hear his defensive words explaining the circumstances, the pain they cause her mother, and the secrecy that must guard the truth: "My father talked and talked and talked; I stopped listening. I had grown up singing about the power of blood. I required no lengthy explanation of what it meant to be adopted. It meant I was not my father's child. It meant I was a secret, even from myself."[11] Therefore, when he steps forward to assume his usual place in the pulpit that summer three years later, she cannot let him claim her as his own, his to forgive. Her actions that summer have demonstrated how far she has departed from his world—the culture of disingenuous, cloying Southern Baptist piety—and she will not let herself be brought back by him. Even though it represents apostasy, and seems to shock even her, her ghostwriting behavior is hers and she will not let him have the last word on it. She is no longer his little girl. He first saw to that, and now she has made it real.

To speak any words, but especially words of forgiveness, is itself an act of power, an act of reclamation, and she demands that act for herself. As she notes in reference to describing the fee schedule for her testimonies, words are worth a great deal: "My prices start at five dollars for words only and go up to twenty dollars for words and concept."[12] Her father, interestingly, is reduced to uncharacteristic silence ("My father never does give a sermon"[13]). Finding himself wordless nevertheless seems to shock him into his first authentic action. His slap, brutal and surprising as it may be, represents a simple, genuine response that contrasts so starkly with all the posturing and dissimulation the story has thus far associated him with. Not only does his slap put him in the vulnerable position, because she is the one to forgive, but it makes him real to the reader for the first time in the narrative. Thus, "authenticity" is defined in this story as being real, being one's own self, saying what you mean, and expressing that in ways that are true to the self one is. If the girl comes across as the heroine, as deeply flawed as her actions are, it is because she is the one making the bravest attempt to be herself. She thinks of something to do that is as bad as keeping adoption a secret, wrests herself free from that legacy, and yet in the end has grown up enough to give herself back to her father as his (now transformed) little girl.

INAUTHENTIC PASTORAL DISCOURSE

Unfortunately, too many of us in the ministry react like Bobby Dunn to the weighty responsibility of saying something authentic when called upon to speak in the name of the Lord. We may know what we want to say, but fear that it will come out all wrong, or worse, we may know there is *nothing* we can say but fear that by saying nothing we will appear incompetent. So we cover our anxiety with words we have borrowed or fabricated, and make them sound profound. We are fairly confident, after all, that few people will detect the difference. Most of our people will never realize the short cuts we take and the insecurity that lies behind them. They trust us, after all, not only to know all about spiritual matters but also to be able to explain them. As moral theologian Richard Gula puts it: "Through diverse functions, pastoral ministers serve as a theological resource for the community by lifting up and living out the word. We are recognized as the ones trained to discern meaning by being both reliable interpreters of the stories of God's presence and action in the world and witnesses to them."[14]

Interpreting the word of God to people thus becomes a matter of ministerial competence. Writing out of the Roman Catholic tradition, Gula is particularly sensitive to the symbolic power that the office of pastoral minister carries and the high expectations people have of it. He also recognizes the projections people place onto those who occupy the pastoral office. They sometimes entrust clergy with power on the basis of little else than the fact that they are clergy (as we saw in the chapter on misconduct). Some even mistake clergy for God. But it would be unfair to dismiss these responses as simply the people's problem. Gula insists that clergy not skirt the expectations laid upon them. If ministers are sometimes granted too much power by an overly trusting flock, they should still try to be as effective communicators of the word as they can be.

This is a great responsibility, and not one easily met. When we consider the job description of most clergy, we see that the bulk of what clergy do is related to what they say. Ministers talk a lot. And by this I do not mean that they are long winded (though many are), but, rather, that their work consists of talking. Preaching, counseling, teaching, meeting people, leading them places, praying with and for them, writing (putting talk on paper), testifying, managing groups, advocating for social change—in all of these exercises of their profession clergy draw upon their ability with words. What ministers have, professionally speaking, are their words, spoken in the name of the one true Word. They do not, for the most part, trade in goods or services, things produced or delivered, but rather in the things communicated. Words are their craft.

Words are also the source of most of the power clergy have at their disposal. Ethicist William F. May makes this point when comparing the powers of clergy to the powers of a head of state:

> The pastor has no troops to command and very minimal power of command over subordinates on the executive side of his or her responsibilities. . . . The more important substantive powers of the presidency lie in the powers of persuasion. In that respect, the powers of the presidential office resemble Athens more than Sparta. Whereas Sparta rested upon the tight-lipped power of command, Athens rested upon the power of the word, the art of persuasion. The *logos* or *rhetor* creates the *polis*; in the absence of the word, a society rests on the noise of weapons, not upon the meaning of words.[15]

But too many ministers still try to lead like commanders-in-chief, attempting to execute orders and manage other people like a Spartan. They forget that persuasive words and rhetoric—in the best sense of that term—are ultimately their most powerful tools.

I think that when clergy realize that "all" they have are their words, the temptation arises to abuse them. Eventually they betray others' trust. When laypeople realize how much stock they have put in the words they have heard from clergy, they are especially dismayed to be let down by false or disingenuous ones. Ministers form their relationships with people by talking to them. People entrust them with the assumption that what they hear will be authentic and true.

Let us consider some ways that ministers let others down by the way they use words. First, there is testimony, as we have seen. The temptation faced by anyone telling his or her faith story in public is to offer a pretentious, drawn-out, inauthentic discourse instead of the truth. Clergy in particular become especially skilled at testimony, even those from non-testimonial traditions. Throughout their formation to become ministers, after all, would-be clergy of all stripes are asked on numerous occasions to share the story of their faith. This may sometimes take the form of an invitation to give actual testimony in public worship, or it may be the "faith journey" or the story of their "call," requested during a church gathering, or simply the answer to the conversational question, "How did you know you wanted to be ordained?" Many laypeople have been learning of late how to tell their faith journeys to each other, but the ordained have always had to have a narrative ready to tell, explaining how their life has led up to the point whereby they are now called by God to minister to others. These call stories can become quite polished. They can also be embellished, or nutshelled, as the occasion demands.[16] They function as a shorthand way to justify a minister's special status.[17] Offered in narrative form, they are meant to make it seem as though everything that happened in the narrator's life prefigured The Call. Sidetracks, doubts, and delays are conveniently downplayed or else worked into the story. The danger is that sometimes ministers' testimony about their call to ministry can start to sound like that of an overly earnest Faith Camper. The importance of sharing an accurate picture of their lives recedes before the importance of trying to live up to some perceived standard of ministerial perfection.

One of the areas of responsibility in the clergy's life where they might be most tempted to abuse words is preaching. After all, both great power and great responsibility come from being in the pulpit, and it is all too easy to turn into someone different while standing there. In typical pulpit architecture, clergy are literally raised up on a platform to offer their words. Even one's own voice can start to sound different. In addition, the words of a sermon are not just the preacher's but based on biblical texts, holy words, the Word. Preaching confers a huge burden on the clergy to say what they mean (and what the text means) and mean what they say, in the name of God. It is a terrifying undertaking. William Willimon quotes the prophet Malachi's warning to clergy: "The lips of a priest should guard knowledge, and people should seek instruction from his mouth, for he is the messenger of the LORD of hosts" (2:7). Willimon recognizes the temptation to bow to this great pressure: "We live in a culture of deceit. In such a time, it is easy to lose our way. Therefore, we preachers would do well to cling to our vocation, to determine to know nothing save that which the church has called us to preach, to serve the Word before we bow before other gods."[18] In order to prevent bowing before the "other gods" of expediency, flattery, and eloquence, Willimon cautions his reader to follow certain "homiletical habits": "disciplined, weekly study; honesty and humility about what the text says and does not say; confidence in the ability of God to make our puny congregations worthy to hear God's Word; a weekly willingness to allow the Word to devastate the preacher before it lays a hand on the congregation . . ."[19]

When preachers neglect these habits, they run the risk of turning into not just a Bobby Dunn but also another fictional character: Elmer Gantry

of Sinclair Lewis's 1927 novel of the same name. Pastoral theologian Gaylord Noyce warns clergy against the temptation to let preaching distort
their ego lest they imitate this infamous character:

> Elmer Gantry, who ended up a corrupt imposter of a parson, was born,
> said Sinclair Lewis, "to be a senator. He never said anything important,
> and he always said it sonorously. He could make 'Good Morning' seem
> profound as Kant, welcoming as a brass band, and uplifting as a cathe-
> dral organ." You and I have met preachers who tried their good mornings
> that way. We have heard insubstantial sermons delivered that way.[20]

Noyce names the preacher's responsibility as one of fidelity.[21] Preachers
must be faithful to preaching's elemental purposes, which Noyce identifies
as proclamation, edification, and invitation. These are not just homiletical
but also ethical imperatives. All preaching must proclaim God's truth and
mercy both explicitly and implicitly, and preaching becomes unfaithful if
it does not.[22] It also has to teach people, conveying truth and knowledge
clearly. The sermon must neither exceed its listeners' intellectual reach nor
underestimate them with its simplicity. "Let there be no hiding behind any
professional cloaks, fostering obscurity for the sake of professional status"
but also, "Pastors who leave their listeners unnecessarily ignorant of tex-
tual criticism in their preaching, for fear of complaints from the congregation, need to supplement the virtue of love with that of courage."[23] Finally,
preaching must invite people into the faith, not by hammering away at
them "the way we drive a nail into a board" but by carefully responding
to people's own lives and stories. One way to do this is for preachers to
admit publicly their own doubt and confusion. Rather than being a show
of weakness, Noyce calls this a form of invitation.[24] One could sum up
Noyce's ethical advice by saying that preachers must take their preaching
very seriously but not themselves. Heeding this distinction would prevent
the anxious Faith Camper inside many preachers from abusing the pulpit
and those in the pews.

The teaching office is closely related to that of preaching and as such
contains a similar temptation to dissimulate. People who trust ministers
trust them to unpack the word of God and relate it to their lives. There
is great authority here, and a corresponding tendency to take too many
liberties with the true meaning of a text or teaching. Noyce complains,
"A preacher will say, 'All the biblical writers insist' when it is not true, or
'Never before in human history' or 'The greatest Christian leader of our

time' when each is doubtful."[25] Sometimes when ministers assume their teaching role, they begin to pontificate and stretch the truth. They gloss over the difficult details and paradoxes of the Christian faith. The hard truths are that the Bible is inconsistent, human history often repeats itself, and no single Christian leader (besides Jesus) could be the greatest. To suggest otherwise is to render the task of interpreting Scripture and tradition too easy. This does a disservice to the people one is trying to teach. It also serves the teachers by letting them off the hook. If the risk of occupying the pulpit is drawing the listeners' attention away from the preaching and onto the preacher, the risk in the classroom is focusing on the teacher rather than the teaching.

To be sure, sometimes clergy attempt not to make things too easy on their students but, rather, too hard. Some try to teach people the way they were taught in seminary—assigning difficult reading, delving into intellectual subtleties, or attempting to cover great swaths of information. In its own way, however, this tendency to make everything "academic" is also a sort of posturing, for it most likely serves the minister's desire to be a great pedagogue more than it does the people's need to learn. Theologian Eugene Peterson recalls his own self-centeredness as a new pastor fresh out of seminary who embraced too heartily his teaching role:

> I had been on an exuberant foray into the country of Scripture and theology in my years of study and was eager to take others on safari with me. I knew I could rescue the Arian controversy from textbook dullness and present the decipherment of Ugaritic in such ways that would enhance appreciation for the subtle elegances of biblical language and story. . . . I had come into the parish seeing its great potential as a learning center, a kind of mini-university in which I was the resident professor.[26]

Peterson came to realize that his congregation wanted to learn, but what they wanted to learn was not how to read Ugaritic but, rather, how to pray. He discovered that to be faithful to the real task of teaching in the church, he needed to convey less information and turn instead to what he calls the "first language" of relationship and devotion. Helping his people cultivate the language of prayer in their spiritual lives was as important as bringing them to the same level of intellectual discourse he had enjoyed as a student. This by no means meant succumbing to anti-intellectualism but, rather, focusing on what was essential and real. He eventually realized that his earlier zeal for educating the congregation had in fact really been a response to his own needs, not theirs. Meeting our own needs is often the reason, I believe, for letting others down.

In the realm of pastoral care, ministers likewise find it all too easy to avoid the real needs of those they would serve. When faced with situations that defy their understanding and challenge their competency, clergy sometimes hide behind their collars. Sometimes they shy away from engaging the situation on the right level. At other times they pretend to know more than they really do about the ways of God and the meaning of suffering. Who among us, after all, can find a truly sufficient word to say when faced with human life at its most tragic? We end up saying the words we think we are supposed to say whether or not we believe them to be true or meaningful. The pressure not to stay silent is simply too great. But failure to honor the reality of human suffering by covering it over with words is an abuse of trust.[27] As Gula puts it, "The trust necessary to sustain the pastoral relationship is based on the confidence that we are competent to address people's religious needs."[28]

Admittedly people's confidence often slides into overconfidence, and they begin to think that the minister has some sort of direct connection to God that they lack. But giving in to this heady sense of authority is a sign of danger. Out come the clichés and the oversimplifications with which we are all too familiar: "It must have been God's will," "Everything happens for a reason," "God won't give you more suffering than you can handle." Such statements, I believe, are uttered primarily in order to placate or impress, not to address the real situation at hand. The speaker in such cases may not have stopped to ponder whether his words correspond to the reality of the other person's need or not. The clichés function to make pastoral care-giving easier and maintain the facade of the authoritative, caring pastor.

Finally, prayer is a pastoral practice that can harm others if done thoughtlessly. Novices to public praying are all too aware of the pressure placed on them to speak to God on behalf of others.[29] They feel like they are imposters. Some of them start to feel better when they have memorized some "stock phrases" and develop some techniques to get them through. This is certainly understandable. "Fake it until you can make it" can be helpful advice to ministers in training who are overly concerned with their performance. The problem is that some will never stop faking it. The real imposters are those who continue to pray by rote, without thinking about the context of the prayer or those for whom it is offered.

Of course, other novices relish the chance to inhabit the pastoral role and offer a blessing or a word of healing. They tend to seize the opportunity go on too long. Noyce describes this kind of pastoral presence: "most of us pray too actively, full of egocentric concern, full of petition, too impatient."[30] It is difficult to get it right. But as Walter Wiest and Elwyn Smith argue in their book on ministry ethics, prayer is too important to entrust to ministers who do not try: "while church and clergy cannot assume responsibility for what people hear, they are responsible for telling the truth. This means not only getting the words right but saying them in contexts that make for understanding rather than misunderstanding or making misunderstanding virtually certain, and by acting in ways that are consistent with the theological understandings that undergird prayer."[31]

TRUTH AND TRUST IN CLERGY

These examples underscore the familiar adage about honesty: at all times you should try to say what you mean and mean what you say. As Williams's story taught us, you should have the courage, first of all, to find out what something means and what it means to you, and then you should say it so that whatever comes out of your mouth is the truth. Wiest and Smith emphasize the importance for clergy of both saying what you mean and meaning what you say. "Truth—which includes both truthfulness and being true—is the key both to ministry and the ethics of ministry."[32] Telling the truth is a cornerstone of ministerial integrity, so the breadth of their definition is especially welcome. Truth means being true as well as telling the truth. For a minister, "being true" means several things. It means, above all, being true to the gospel message. It also means establishing relationship. "Truth means being open to others. There can be no genuine community between false selves."[33] Being true also means upholding the standards of the ministerial profession. It is important that ministers of the gospel aim for excellent professional performance. "We have a responsibility to do an honest job, which means acquiring the necessary knowledge and skills and being on our honor to use them well."[34]

Wiest and Smith's insistence that ministers always do an honest job, as simple as that may sound, opens the way for us to consider truth in the ministry as a matter of professional trust. Recall that we have defined trust as accepted vulnerability to possible harm. It may not initially seem that failing to say what you mean or mean what you say counts as a betrayal of trust. Some of the examples given above may not appear to make anyone overly vulnerable or take power away from anyone—the moral features of trust we have thus far been looking for. Relishing the authority of one's position, glossing over a few details, or even borrowing a few words here and there may not appear to put anyone at risk of vulnerability to harm or take power away from anyone—the moral features of trust we have thus far been looking for. Is pastoral speech really a grave trust issue? It is certainly true that on the larger scale of things, there are worse violations of trust and worse things that clergy can do to inflict harm upon their flock. But violations of honesty *are* violations of professional trust because people who have entrusted themselves to you deserve your good faith in return.

Of course, it is not only the clergy who should be honest. The ethics of truth telling has a long and solid history. Unlike some issues in Christian and professional ethics, systematic attention to the morality of lying goes back a long way, at least as far back as Augustine. Therefore, it is not new to say that telling the truth is right and lying is wrong. Nor is it novel to point out the contradiction between lying and the trustworthy practice of ministry. Nevertheless, it may be useful very briefly to remind ourselves of the reasons against lying and the reasons, in particular, why lies undermine trust. Then we will be in a better position to evaluate why speech acts short of lying, like bullshit, undermine trust as well.

A lie is a false statement uttered with the intention of deceiving someone about something. Liars are self-centered and often selfish. As ethicist Paul Griffiths describes the Augustinian view of lying: "the liar takes control of her speech, and marks it as her own when she separates it from her thought and grants it autonomy. When this is done, speech becomes the possession and instrument of the speaker."[35] But lies also always presuppose a relationship. We may not think of lying in a relational sense, but a lie would not work if the liar did not have someone to tell it to who would believe the duplicity. Usually a liar has a purpose they need to achieve for which they need the cooperation of others. For example, Williams's protagonist wants to get back at her father so she needs her audience to hear her "confession." Sometimes a liar has a relationship to maintain that the exposure of truth would interfere with, so he tells an untruth in order that others will be steered away from whatever is factually the case. Liars by definition do not seek advance approval for their lies (though they may anticipate having to seek forgiveness afterward). They instead presume that in their relationship they will be believed. In other words, they presume the trust of the deceived to pull off their intentions.

Because relationships are stake, liars run risks. Some of the risks are similar to those we saw with the gossiper—of the target finding out, of being exposed in shameful behavior, and so on. Liars also run the risk that they will have to keep on lying. Frequently they have to spin an entire "web of deceit" because one lie is seldom enough to achieve their goal. Perhaps the most significant risk liars take, however, is with their own moral integrity. As Immanuel Kant argued better than anyone else, liars violate their own reason by resorting to lies and thus their dignity as moral beings. "For the dishonor (being an object of moral contempt) that accompanies a lie also accompanies a liar like his shadow. . . . By a lie a man throws away and, as it were, annihilates his dignity as a man."[36]

Lying is a relational act just like entrusting, only it is opposite. Before trust is bestowed, Person B decides to go ahead and take something valuable from Person A. A entrusts B in the very general sense of agreeing to the tacit rules of human conversation, but the trust is not really freely bestowed because A never has a choice. The "Valued Thing C" taken from A is no less than the capacity to reason. Kantian philosopher Christine Korsgaard has written that in lying, "your reason is worked like a machine: the deceiver tries to determine what levers to pull to get the desired results from you. Physical coercion treats someone's person as a tool; lying treats someone's reason as a tool."[37] Another Kantian, jurist and law scholar Charles Fried, puts it even more bluntly: "When I lie, I lay claim to your mind."[38] Fried also describes lying as a relational act: "Lying is wrong because when I lie I set up a relation which is essentially exploitative. It violates the principle of respect, for I must affirm that the mind of another person is available to me in a way in which I cannot agree that my mind would be available to him."[39]

Therefore, lying is a classic violation of trust, as we are analyzing it, because it perverts or exploits the relationship that forms the heart of trust. The deceived bears the bulk of the risk of vulnerability to harm. Theirs is a double risk. Not only are those lied to frequently the ones who suffer whatever consequences come of lies, but they were helpless to prevent the consequences in the first place. This is why Kant argued that as a moral action, lying ranked even worse than physical violence: "All expedients which take us off our guard are thoroughly mean. Such are lying, assassination, and poisoning. To attack a man on the highway is less vile than to attempt to poison him. In the former case, he can at least defend himself, but, as he must eat, he is defenseless against the poisoner."[40] By extension, people are defenseless against liars because they have no choice but to listen and they cannot see the lie coming.

Being lied to renders you vulnerable, even though you may not realize it, for reasons that follow from what we have already said. You are used as a means rather than an end, the classic violation of the Kantian categorical imperative of morality. However benign the circumstances or motivations may be, it remains the case that the liar uses you to fulfill her own purposes. One might argue that the truth is purposeful, too, and that telling the truth can thus in a way be "coercive" as well. But most philosophers, and I think most of the rest of us, recognize a moral difference between the coercion of the truth and that of a lie. While truth may be powerful, it is not coercive in the sense of wresting something away from us. As Griffiths puts it: "Lies require effort; truth none."[41] In a world assumed to be free of deceit, a lie is a deliberate departure. (This is why Kant held liars accountable for *all* the consequences of their lies, however unforeseeable.[42])

The relationship between lying and trust becomes even more clear after the fact of a lie. Many have pointed to the disintegration of trust that lying causes, but Augustine perhaps put it best when he said: "When regard for the truth has been broken down or even slightly weakened, all things will remain doubtful, and unless these are believed to be true, they cannot be considered as certain."[43] When we are told enough lies (and, depending on the severity, it need be only one), we begin to doubt everything we hear. Our habit shifts, as Augustine points out, from one of belief to one of uncertainty or disbelief. We lose confidence in the person we are listening to, and maybe others as well. Liars can drag innocent colleagues down with them. This is one of the most damaging consequences to ordinary parishioners, who are not themselves direct victims, when clergy are caught in a scandal of deception and cover-up. It is nearly impossible to get people to start believing in them again.

WHAT IS BULLSHIT?

If we therefore accept the premise that lies are generally destructive of trust between people, what about the sort of statements that fall short of lying but are less than fully honest? If a lie is a false statement told with the intention to deceive, it has several variants. There is "Jesus Jaw." An inability to express what you want to say is a linguistic problem rather than a moral one, but moral problems arise when those with Jesus Jaw attempt to compensate through some form of dishonesty. There are false statements that are not necessarily factually untrue but nevertheless have the effect of steering the hearer away from the truth. There are things people say without the conscious intention of deceiving others but with so little concern for veracity that the truth often ends up being misrepresented anyway. Gossip fits in this category. And finally, there are utterances meant to persuade, convince, impress, or placate the listener, in which the end becomes more important than the means. While the end may not be deception, neither is it truthfulness. We could put here the growing phenomenon of "spin," to which we are all increasingly subjected. I would argue that these various categories of speech—all these variants on the lie—are as worthy of our moral attention as lying if only because they are so prevalent. And, like gossip, they are harmful precisely because they seem so harmless.

This is what philosopher Harry Frankfurt thought. In 1986, he first published an essay that he called simply "On Bullshit," where he proposed that we take a more serious look at this form of untruthfulness. "One of the most salient features of our culture," he wrote of American society, "is that there is so much bullshit. Everyone knows this."[44] And yet, nearly two decades later, Frankfurt apparently felt the culture of bullshit had, if anything worsened; in any event, he published the essay again in book form.[45]

Frankfurt begins by acknowledging that philosophical inquiry into bullshit is rare and that his contribution will not therefore be definitive. Reminiscent of what we found with the scholarly study of gossip, he writes: "Even the most basic and preliminary questions about bullshit remain, after all, not only unanswered but unasked."[46] Nevertheless, he proceeds on the assumption that most people agree there is such a thing as bullshit and it can be defined. He starts with an example that many in our culture would find familiar, a political speech delivered on the Fourth of July.

> Consider a Fourth of July orator who goes on bombastically about "our great and blessed country, whose Founding Fathers under divine guidance created a new beginning for mankind." . . . The orator is not lying. He would be lying only if it were his intention to bring about in his audience beliefs that he himself regards as false, concerning such matters as whether our country is great, whether it is blessed, whether the Founders had divine guidance, and whether what they did was in fact to create a new beginning for mankind. But the orator does not really care what his audience thinks about the Founding Fathers, or about the role of the deity in our country's history, or the like. . . . What he cares about is what people think of *him*.[47]

As this example shows, bullshit is characterized by overblown speech, especially caused by the pretensions of the speaker (hence the description of the speech as "bombastic"). The Founding Fathers did not just make a new start, but were uniquely blessed with the guidance of divinity. By invoking the country's founders, moreover, the speaker seems to seek to align himself with them. One can easily imagine that such a speech would go on in such a way as to tie the speaker to positions that he thinks they would take were they only here today. Many of us, I believe, when we think of "bullshit" think of precisely the kind of posturing and claim to grandiosity this speaker makes. But for Frankfurt that still does not quite get at its essence.

Two other features are also important. On the one hand, the bullshitter is not saying whatever comes to mind. He *does* care what his audience thinks. His words are in that sense carefully chosen. The politician, above, knows that certain phrases and cultural references will warm the audience to him in the way he wants. Bullshitters often have stock phrases, even stock speeches, that they utilize again and again because those phrases and speeches succeed for them in producing what they want. On the other hand, the bullshitter's talk is not really careful, in the sense of being conscientious. The Fourth of July politician does not want to become ensnared in questions of whether God was really on the side of the country's founders— or now endorses the politician's particular goals—so he makes vague reference to "divine guidance." There is a certain laziness about what bullshitters do, and this is why we so often associate it with rambling, leisurely talk. A study of the word's etymological roots yields close connections to excrement, obviously, and also hot air or vapor, all of which are vapid and empty of meaningful content. Bullshit is non-sense; the words themselves have little value or sense-making substance. It is a kind of talk that is easy to blow off or produce and is not supposed to be taken seriously for what it contains.[48]

This curious combination of caring but not caring epitomizes bullshit. The best way to put it is that the bullshitter is trying to get away with something. He has an end in mind but is not devoted to the work of getting there. People try to "get away" with things precisely when they cannot or do not want to put in the effort it would otherwise require of them to do a complete and decent job.[49] Politicians bullshit because they have the end of getting elected uppermost in mind. (To be fair, the demands exerted by the media for quick, sound-bite truths also make it very difficult for politicians to offer the public any comprehensive explanations of their positions. Between the industries of politics and advertising we the people are exposed to more bullshit than from almost any other source.) The campers at Faith Camp were trying to get away with delivering effective testimonies without working at it themselves, so they hired a writer. They cared what their audience thought—perhaps even too much—but did not care enough to expend the effort. If for no other reason than this shoddy approach to relationship, bullshit should be considered a breach of trust.

Beyond this, bullshit is deceptive. It may be pretentious and lazy, and it may not count as a full lie, but as Frankfurt argues, bullshit *is* misrepresentation. What the bullshitter misrepresents are not necessarily the facts. As the example above shows, the Fourth of July orator does not misstate or lie about any truths. Rather, he gives a false impression of his enterprise. He does not care what his audience thinks of American history, despite what all the words coming out of his mouth suggest. We might even question whether he cares what his audience thinks about the issues at hand for that day. "What he cares about is what people think of *him*." *This* endeavor is what the bullshitter misrepresents, for he does not actually talk about himself at all. The words he says probably refer to issues and ideas and sentiments about America. It might not be easy for some to detect his real purpose, which is to make an impression by associating himself with those ideas. But bullshit is about disguising that purpose.

Therefore, bullshit *is* deceptive, if in a different way. *The difference between a liar and a bullshitter is that a liar deliberately steers people away from the truth while a bullshitter does not care what the truth is.* He, like the liar, wants to steer people somewhere, but the relation of that end to the truth is immaterial. The nonrelationship between bullshit's content and the truth is what is deceiving.

Frankfurt draws a good analogy between bullshit and forgery. Like a piece of art that has been forged, bullshit can seem quite impressive. It can be hard for people to tell whether it is the "real thing," an original produced by a serious artist, or not. Usually there are holes in the story, so to speak, that give the process away, but the bullshitter puts up a convincing appearance. The key difference between a forgery and an original, then, is not so much the final product but the process.

For the essence of bullshit is not that it is false but that it is phony. In order to appreciate this distinction, one must recognize that a fake or a phony need not be in any respect (apart from authenticity itself) inferior to the real thing. What is not genuine need not also be defective in some other way. It may be, after all, an exact copy. What is wrong with a counterfeit is not what it is like, but how it was made.[50]

How bullshit gets made is the heart of the matter for Frankfurt. A liar sticks close to the truth, at least in her mind, in order the better to mislead people. We could even say that liars honor veracity. They need to be concerned with what is true so that they can craft a good lie. The bullshitter is just the opposite. The bullshitter does not care about what is true. Reference to an exact copy notwithstanding, the bullshitter will use anything to get through. This can and may very well include the truth. This is what Frankfurt means by the difference between something false and something fake. Bullshit need not be false any more than it need be true. It mixes veracity and falsity at leisure. It simply does not matter whether it is real and can be made one way or the other. The bullshitter just "picks [things] out, or makes them up, to suit his purpose."[51]

This is what makes bullshit so insidious to Frankfurt. It is important, he argues, to care about what side of the truth you are on. A liar is preferable to a bullshitter because at least the liar picks a side. The bullshitter's utter disregard for authenticity is worse than the liar's falsehoods.

Frankfurt's vehement critique of bullshit explains, finally, why the campers' fake testimonies are worse than the girl's less than fully truthful confession in "Personal Testimony." As questionable as her actions are, at least the girl knows her purpose. She stays on one side of the truth and uses it. She writes testimonies for money, and eventually confesses to this behavior, in order to get even with a father who himself hid the truth of his daughter's parentage from her. As I argued earlier, her actions are the most authentic ones of the story. *She* is not a phony. She cares deeply about the truth—the truth of her adoption and her father's deception, and the truth of the young woman she is becoming. The other campers, in contrast, are Frankfurt's bullshitters. They do not care *what* they say in front of others. They seek false standards of perfection, they are pretentious and ambitious, and they will not let the truth get in their way. At the same time, they are lazy. They cannot take the time to write their own testimonies. If they did not have a ghostwriter, they would probably be happy to forge them from someone else's. They are simply hoping to make an impression and it does not particularly matter to them how accurate it is. They have been steeped in the culture of Faith Camp, which prizes the appearance of piety over the virtue of sincerity.

THE PURPOSE OF BULLSHIT

Frankfurt does not write much about those on the receiving end of bullshit, but I would argue that our sense of outrage can be as bad when we hear bullshit as when we are lied to. If bullshitters do not care about the truth, neither can they care about relationship. Therefore, they harm and insult us. Bullshit is also bewildering, for as a listener you are simultaneously trying to figure out which words you are hearing to believe and trying to assess the sincerity of the one talking. Bullshit is a lot like gossip in that it happens within a context of suspended reality. The bullshitter disclaims the truth of what he is saying. Unlike gossip, however, where everyone participating usually buys into the suspension of veracity, the bullshitter takes advantage of the ambiguity. If the gossiper wants to be shielded from accountability for what she says, the bullshitter also wants to be shielded—but in this case from the authenticity of what he says. The "target" of bullshit knows *who* is saying potentially false things, and sometimes likely knows *why*, but probably does not know *what* may be false and what true. This is a different position to be in than either the dupe of a lie or the target of gossip—it is sort of in the middle—but equally difficult. In the terms with which we are now familiar, bullshit makes the hearer vulnerable to the power words carry to convey a message. If the message is inauthentic and delivered without care, whether or not it is also ambiguous or unclear, the power of the words is difficult to deflect. If the authenticity of the message is itself in doubt, then the listener cannot trust anything she hears. She is put at a distinct disadvantage any time she has to listen. This strains her relationship with the one talking, and trust is eroded. If it eventually becomes clear that the message is only intended to impress her and really communicates more about the one speaking than about her, she may withdraw any trust she ever bestowed.

So why would people of faith engage in bullshit? While we have argued that, like the campers who desperately want to appear more devout than they really are, ministers who shoot the bull are trying to assume a fake posture, we have not exactly defined the function of bullshit in the pastoral context. To become clearer about bullshit in the ministry, however, is to become clearer about ministerial power and its excess.

When we discussed gossip, we saw that its defenders mainly based their arguments on the functions it performs. Gossip was thought to promote social bonding, maintain community standards, facilitate the flow of information, and so on. We agreed that gossip did indeed fulfill such needs within communities, even communities of faith, but we argued that there were other ways to do the same thing without the pernicious effects. Unlike with gossip, with bullshit we have no studies, psychological or otherwise, to go on. We are left with speculation. But we may nevertheless ask some of the same questions we did with gossip.

The one scholar I know of who has studied bullshit in a professional context is philosopher G. A. Cohen. Cohen wrote an essay in 2002 entitled "Deeper Into Bullshit" as a response to Harry Frankfurt's original essay. It was published in a volume of essays that honored Frankfurt's career and is one of the only formal, published responses to "On Bullshit."[52] Cohen does not take on bullshit throughout American society, the way Frankfurt had, just in academia (where, nevertheless, one can find a lot of it). Cohen's focus is on evaluating the act of bullshit itself, not necessarily the bullshitter's intention, on which Frankfurt had almost exclusively focused. So he considers the actual *content* of various kinds of bullshit across a range of contexts. He comes up with the following list of essential descriptors: the content of bullshit is *nonsensical, unclarifiable, unintelligible, obscure,* and/or *irretrievably speculative.*[53] This is why it is wrong. Bullshit is by its nature deceptive speech, even if it falls short of lying, because no one but the bullshitter can engage it and make sense of it. It is "unclarifiable unclarity." When a scholar claims, "People today think about sex more than they did one hundred years ago," there is simply no way to test such a claim, and it becomes irretrievably speculative (if nevertheless plausible and thus convincing).[54] Examples in academic prose, Cohen argues, abound. Academics make claims that no one else can clarify.

Academics communicate this way out of a selfish need to sound erudite. Sometimes they fake knowledge because it makes them look more learned among their colleagues than they really are. Sometimes the pressure from nonacademics to sound educated and expert in one's field is genuine, and academics give in to it. Sometimes the support simply does not exist for a claim they really want to make and think is right, so they make it anyway. But it is wrong for academics to talk and write in ways that nobody can understand nor even render understandable. Doing so might be a source of great pride to them but represents a real barrier to meaningful academic discourse. If nobody, even within a scholar's own discipline, can understand the scholar's work, there can be no real exchange or critique of ideas. No one else can make intelligible something only intelligible to its author.

When it comes to pastoral bullshit, I think sometimes it shares with academic bullshit the function of unclarifiable unclarity, but just as often I think something else is at play. Cohen may think the hallmarks of bullshit are its unintelligibility, obscurity, and irretrievable speculation, but I think it is just as likely that bullshit can take the form of certitude. In other words, might not bullshit also function to make things clearer than they really are, simpler than they ought to be, easier than they seem? I believe so. *I think the purpose of pastoral bullshit is to make assertions that are unassailable.* This is why we find pastoral bullshit in preaching, teaching, and prayer—the realms where clergy assert the Christian faith.

Frankfurt notes that bullshit is frequently exchanged in group settings called "bull sessions." A bull session is a conversation among buddies who tacitly agree not to take the conversation too seriously and thus enjoy the freedom of expression that comes when the normal rules of conversation are suspended. Participants can float outrageous comments or just vent ("shoot the bull").

> What tends to go on in a bull session is that the participants try out various thoughts and attitudes in order to see how it feels to hear themselves saying such things and in order to discover how others respond, without it being assumed that they are committed to what they say. . . . Therefore provision is made for enjoying a certain irresponsibility, so that people will be encouraged to convey what is on their minds without too much anxiety that they will be held to it.[55]

The bull session is like the gossip session. Both function as a context for a kind of talk that will never see the light of day. Like gossipers, bullshitters make use of linguistic devices to embellish or disclaim what they are saying. They exaggerate and introduce deliberate obfuscation. If gossipers use standard lines like "Now, don't repeat this, but . . . ," a standard bullshitting line is something like, "Now, of course you all know that . . . " Both gossip and bullshit allow the circulation of illicit or sensitive conversation topics. Frankfurt even points out that bull sessions "have to do with very personal and emotion-laden aspects of life—for instance, religion, politics, or sex," which is similar, as we saw, to the content of gossip.[56] In current parlance, we might say that both gossip and bull sessions allow people to say things that would otherwise be "politically incorrect."

I would argue, however, that for the most part the similarities between the bull session and the gossip clique end there. The relative social location of the participants—vis-à-vis one another and those not present—is different. We said earlier that gossip is triadic. Gossipers come together and collude with one another to talk about a third person who is absent. Bullshit is not necessarily structured the same way. In fact, the bull session has no particular relational structure at all that I can see, other than people coming together to talk. And bullshitters do not even so much talk about others as they do about themselves. Bullshit is—as we have said in one way or another throughout this chapter—a self-centered activity. If bullshitters collude, I would argue, it is simply to let each other take the spotlight for a moment. In addition, we saw that with gossip, cliques tend to center around some people more than others. The same gossipers talk more, initiate more topics, and seem subtly to control the flow of the discourse. Whether bull sessions have similar leaders or are instead more democratic and egalitarian is anyone's guess. I would surmise that in a bull session there are those who "get away with" more bullshit than others but that no one particularly tries to control its flow.

Gossip is tied to social location in that gossiping activity itself is organized around—and organizes—the relative social stature of those gossiping. There are those who are "in" and those who are "out." Gossip reinforces social power even in the way the discourse gets structured. This is why it is a tool of the relatively powerless, like girls and women in a male-dominated society. Bullshit, on the other hand, may be tied to social location but the relevant status, I suspect, is that of individual speaker to individual listener. It is not as thoroughly a communal activity as gossip, the concept of the bull "session" notwithstanding. It is all about the one doing the talking gaining and maintaining the attention of others. We saw this in the example of the Fourth of July politician. We can even, in our mind's eye, conjure the body language bullshitters use. If the image associated with gossip is of someone leaning in to whisper something to others, the image of bullshit is someone puffed up and talking away but making no eye contact.

I would argue that bullshit is a male phenomenon. After all, the word itself supports this. The word *bullshit* refers, of course, to the waste product of a male bovine. I think it is no coincidence, moreover, that we associate men with the bull session the way we associate women with the gossip clique. We conceded that when it came to gossip, women probably do engage in it more than men. Gossip is both a stereotype and a reality of women's lives. We hypothesized that women gossip because gossip is a tool of the powerless to gain some measure of power. Among other things, it is an outlet for impermissible aggression, a sort of passive-aggressive behavior of those who do not want to or cannot express their thoughts directly.

Gossip is also a safe way to test out certain ideas or opinions, especially novel or potentially scandalous ones. But bullshit is an outlet for those who are allowed freely to express themselves (even though they may not think they are able to do so very well). Bullshitters take advantage of the implicit permission—and even high regard—that other people grant them. They engage in bullshit because they can. It is a way not so much to test out ideas but to control other people's ideas of them. It is not necessarily passively aggressive but passively manipulative. Therefore, I would hypothesize that men bullshit because *bullshit is a tool of the powerful to maintain the power they have been granted but fear losing.* Bullshit functions for men the way gossip functions for women.

This is why in the context of the church I write about gossip with respect to parishioners and bullshit with respect to clergy. Clergy bullshit because theirs is the more privileged position within the church, especially when it comes to the power of using words on others. Associating laity with gossip and clergy with bullshit is a very rough division, of course, as is the association of gender with each. Clearly ministers gossip and laypeople bullshit just as women engage in bullshit and men in gossip. My point is that these are behaviors associated with relative degrees of power. If an ordained person has less relative power, like many associate ministers, then they might gossip about their superiors. Powerful lay leaders might, correspondingly, use their position in the church to bullshit.

If my hypothesis about bullshit and power is correct, then members of the clergy need to bullshit because they need to maintain the power they are given. If they are supposed to have the ear and mouth of God and fear they do not, they must make it sound as though they do. Pastors attempt to simplify and demystify the Christian faith when they feel too burdened to tease out its complexities, too frightened to be bearers of a mystery. Clergy are made to think their role is to make the faith clear and accessible, to win people to it, and that to them alone falls the task of being an apologist for it. This is why I argue that pastoral bullshit is composed of unassailable assertions. But like the campers at Faith Camp, it is hard to be seen as less pious than people suppose clergy to be. It is very difficult to admit not having all the answers, or at least the right words to say. So clergy say what comes most easily to mind. Clergy know that people listen to them and they find this fact both scary *and* seductive. Unable to reconcile these contradictory aspects of having been invested with such authority, clergy sometimes resort to bullshit. They abandon the struggle of searching with care for words and instead forge statements that sound good. They end up using words in an attempt to shore up the fragile power that having only words confers.

In conclusion, the ethics of pastoral bullshit are closely connected to the ethics of pastoral power.[57] If we would accept the entrustment of others to speak to them honestly about things that matter, we must keep in mind that being trusted this way is extraordinarily powerful. The more the topic matters (say, the death of a child or a nation going to war) the more powerful our role becomes, for we are being entrusted to render it meaningful. People entrust clergy to interpret what they cannot by themselves interpret. They give over to clergy their comprehension of things that are, often, incomprehensible. But ultimately they want honesty, not unassailable assertions. Clergy who shirk their power in this regard and offer bullshit instead of an authentic response are effectively breaching the trust relationship. As Willimon says, "The church is full of much harm done by powerful people who refuse to acknowledge how much they are able to hurt other people."[58]

When it comes to bullshit, they may not be immediately "caught." Bullshit is unlike lying, lacking as it does a clear motive and intended consequences. It is not even like gossip, lacking a specified target. But a trust relationship does exist, and bullshit does violate it. I would argue that if we consider the profession of ministry as a whole, bullshit accounts for a great deal of the skepticism and downright dissatisfaction people have toward clergy. People eventually see through the ruse of faked authority, and once tarnished, authority is difficult to reclaim. As we have said throughout this study, it is easier to establish trust than it is to reestablish it. Once betrayed, people will only slowly make themselves vulnerable again to power.

The good news is that clergy can unlearn the practice of bullshit as they learn new ways to exercise power. Willimon wrote: "We clergy know enough about our roles to know that they put us in risky positions where power is being used and therefore potentially abused, but we don't know enough about how to change our professional practices to improve our profession."[59] Hopefully, by examining here the temptation to bullshit, we have made a start.

❧ CONCLUSION

After listening to me preach in chapel one day, one of my students came up to me and said, "You always like to prick a balloon." This book has been intentionally, though I hope not excessively, provocative. To conclude it, therefore, I would like to share the last word with my imagined reader. Thank you for reading this far. In this dialogue I try to anticipate some of the objections and remaining questions you might have.[1]

Q: *Despite the fact that this is a book on ministry, you don't make many theological or biblical references. What biblical images inform your view of trust?*

A: When it comes to interpersonal trust between individuals, I have always been inspired by the metaphor in Genesis 2 of Adam and Eve in the Garden of Eden. There the couple is described as being "naked but not ashamed." So, before the fall, their relationship to one another was characterized by difference but not domination, exposure but not shame, vulnerability but not exploitation. To be able to be vulnerable before one another, and have that vulnerability be a source of strength rather than a source of fear or enmity, is to me a very powerful image of what it could mean to trust one another. And this story affirms that it was the way we were created to be by God!

For a metaphor of communal life, I draw upon the Pauline image of the body in 1 Corinthians 12. We all need each other and cannot dispense with our "weaker" parts or glorify our more "respectable" ones. Therefore, it would seem that we must find a way to live in community that honors our mutual and ongoing interdependence.

Finally, in all things I depend on the Bible's witness to an eschatological vision of community where worldly powers are reversed and justice reigns.

Q: *Isn't trust between people similar to trust (or faith) in God?*

A: Yes and no. In describing trust, I also look to the biblical stories about the promises or covenants God made with humankind because I think they inform our own covenants with each other. However, the two kinds of covenants are not necessarily parallel. God may be able to love us unconditionally, and therefore we should try to love one another that way, but often we have to place conditions on our covenants with each other. This may be true if only because one "condition" for the true fulfillment of a covenant with someone else is that they make and keep the same covenant with us, and as we know this is unfortunately not always the case.

Q: *Why don't you offer more guidance for when confidences should be broken? Isn't this the minister's primary moral dilemma?*

A: As far as dilemmas go, it probably is. I have tried, however, to shift our attention away from this problem, as difficult as it may be, toward the problem of when we should accept confidences in the first place.

Q: *In chapter 3 you give a strong endorsement for disciplinary procedures as a means of preventing ministerial misconduct. In contrast, you do not give much endorsement at all to various other preventive procedures, like rules of conduct. Can you explain your positions? Why not put procedures in place that will help people act in trustworthy ways, and then extend forgiveness to those who make mistakes? Would not this approach better foster trust between people in the church?*

A: I am not sure how true the saying is that "It's easier to ask for permission than forgiveness." In some communities I know, it actually seems pretty easy to ask for forgiveness, to the extent that I'm not sure people don't figure in, at some level, the ease of being forgiven when taking action. This is a matter of moral psychology, perhaps, and will vary by culture. I also do not mean to say that forgiveness is not important. Leaders who refuse to forgive small mistakes do not promote confidence among those they lead and are less likely to be entrusted in the long run.

As for procedures, I do not necessarily think that trustworthiness will be promoted by setting a lot of parameters for conduct and checking to be sure they are followed. This seems to me to send a message that bad behavior is anticipated. On the contrary, I have always had faith that setting the moral bar high will call forth trustworthy behavior, the same way teachers who expect their students to earn As in fact produce students who earn As. When it comes to volunteers in the church, I am far more in favor of defining their positions very clearly, offering high-quality training, making it clear that these are important roles of which much is expected, and then letting people exercise those roles in an environment relatively free from scrutiny.

I am reminded of the time I served on a committee in an educational institution that was considering implementing an honor code. Some schools have instituted very thorough honor codes, with students and faculty seriously entrusted to be "on their honor" at all times. When exams are given, for example, they are not proctored or even necessarily timed. Often it is in these same schools that the penalty for violating the honor code is high, so that, for example, a student caught cheating will automatically fail the class (or some other penalty). Faculty and students are not allowed to "work things out" between them, but review boards are quickly convened and their decisions trusted. The honor code is highly publicized, ritualized, and well understood within the community; the code itself serves as sufficient warning. I promoted such an honor code within our committee, and it became known as the "high trust, high penalty" approach. While the committee eventually agreed to recommend the implementation of such a code to the faculty, it became a hard sell. Many faculty members at our institution were used to exams where students were not allowed to bring anything into the exam room, were made to sit several seats apart, and where teaching assistants kept an eye on them. It was difficult for them to relinquish these procedures (what I call "audits" in chapter 3). On the other hand, it was also challenging for them to consider a disciplinary procedure that did not appear to have enough opportunities for redemption. It simply seemed too harsh to impose strict penalties so soon, and they preferred a system of warnings and informal processes for handling complaints. An honor code was never implemented. This experience was a valuable lesson to me in the different ways people understand "trust" and the depth of cultural resistance to changing the ways people work toward trustworthiness.

Q: *In chapter 4 you criticize several theologians for their support of gossip. Might they simply be talking about a different phenomenon than you are?*

A: Yes, that certainly might be the case. Gossip is notoriously difficult to define. They do call what they are writing about "gossip" so I take them at face value. The ultimate point, though, is not to criticize certain thinkers but to challenge the church to raise the moral bar on the way we talk about each other.

Q: *You seem to take great pains to offer a balanced view of gossip. What do you* really *think of it?*

A: Before I wrote that chapter, I thought that gossip inevitably destroyed trust and had little redeeming value. My position still remains pretty close to this! However, I wanted to take seriously the "rehabilitation" of gossip that I seemed to be encountering in several places. In addition, when I talked to my friends and colleagues, quite a few of them expressed ambivalence about whether gossip was necessarily wrong. Therefore, I decided that the moral ambiguity surrounding gossip was itself interesting and worth addressing.

In the interim, the case of the Hooksett Four made national news. Cited in chapter 1, this case involved four female office workers in Hooksett, New Hampshire, who were fired for gossiping about their male boss. This case generated discourse about gossip, on all sides. Apparently many people could identify with a longsuffering worker for whom a little office gossip is a way of getting even with The Man. Others thought it was about time that gossip was taken seriously as an ethical problem. Still others noted the gendered power dynamics of the case.

As a feminist, I have become increasingly disturbed by girls' and women's vicious use of gossip and think it needs to be viewed as a product of sexism.

Q: *In contrast, you seem overly sanguine about testimony.*

A: Students and colleagues from traditions where testimony is common have warned me about this! In courses I teach, I invite students to develop an ethic for a practice of testimony in their own church, taking into account such questions as: whether or not testimony should be spontaneous or reviewed ahead of time, whether anyone at all should be allowed to give testimony, and whether content guidelines should be issued. One time a student offered the idea that testimony should always retain its original connection to expressing the *pain* of personal experience, redeemed by God. Otherwise, it runs the risk of simply becoming an opportunity to brag.

Q: *Is it possible to stop a vicious practice of gossip?*

A: If my hypothesis is correct, then gossipers are power-hungry people, and power is not always a bad thing—especially for the powerless. If gossipers could be organized and their hunger for power directed in constructive rather than destructive ways, imagine the possibilities for change!

Q: *Are people surprised to hear that you have written about* bullshit?

A: Only for a moment. I am the one who is always surprised at how readily people can offer me examples of it, even from the ministry.

Notes

1. THE PRACTICE OF TRUST

1. Brian Moore, *The Colour of Blood* (London: Harper Collins, 1994), 39.

2. Ibid., 51.

3. Ibid., 69.

4. Ibid., 105.

5. Ibid., 154.

6. Ibid., 159.

7. For the sake of readers who might want to read *The Colour of Blood* themselves, I will not reveal the ending!

8. Annette Baier, *Moral Prejudices: Essays on Ethics* (Cambridge, Mass.: Harvard University Press, 1994), 98.

9. The dilemma at the heart of this game can be framed without reference to criminality and confession, in case these obscure the morality of trust. The Prisoner's Dilemma has been used to study human cooperation in many realms, from warfare to business practices.

10. From each individual prisoner's point of view, the most profitable thing to do is to betray because this choice could mean freedom. Many theorists thus argue that the rational and self-interested choice is betrayal and conclude that a reasonable person playing this game would always choose Betray. However, if the prisoners choose against their own self-interest *and* trust each other both to do the same, they will maximize the outcome for both. The game would therefore seem to contain a paradox: choosing self-interest can result in becoming worse off than choosing cooperation. Or, to put it in popular terms, Nice Guys Can Finish First. In 1984, Robert Axelrod used the Prisoner's Dilemma to mount an argument for the evolution of altruistic behavior. Robert M. Axelrod, *The Evolution of Cooperation* (New York: Basic Books, 1984).

11. In what follows I am indebted to Annette Baier's essays on trust.

12. B also has to accept the ambiguity of not knowing how jealous A will become regarding C.

13. Niklas Luhmann, *Trust and Power* (New York: Wiley, 1979), 13.

14. Writing when he did, Luhmann probably did not anticipate the "information age" and the exponential growth of information both true and false that we now have to reckon with in our daily lives.

15. Sometimes especially when we are under stress, we are tempted to intervene with this kind of decisive measure. In an infamous case of office gossip in New Hampshire in 2007, a boss who suspected that his workers had been trading

nasty rumors about him hired a fact-finder to ferret out the source of the gossip and then used the evidence to fire them. As it turned out, they countered his retaliation by garnering attention in the national press. Not only did the so-called Hooksett Four gain sympathy, but by getting their story out so widely, they drew only more attention to the very rumors their boss had hoped to quash. The moral of this story seems to be that checking up on those you are supposed to trust can backfire on you and make an already poor trust relationship even worse. See Emil Steiner, "Free Speech, Employment Law and the Hooksett 4: Can You Be Fired for Gossiping About Your Boss?" http://blog.washingtonpost.com/offbeat/2007/05/free_speech_employment_law_and.html, May 24, 2007, accessed April 7, 2008.

16. Luhmann, *Trust and Power,* 14.

17. Ibid., 26.

18. In public life, driving in traffic is often cited as an example of trust. But is it accurate to say that we trust other drivers, or are we simply relying on the sanctions they will incur if they ignore the rules of the road?

19. Baier, *Moral Prejudices,* 100, 158.

20. Diego Gambetta, ed., *Trust: Making and Breaking Cooperative Relations* (New York: Basil Blackwell, 1988) as cited in ibid., 187.

21. Baier, *Moral Prejudices,* 117.

22. Edmund D. Pellegrino, "Trust and Distrust in Professional Ethics," in *Ethics, Trust and the Professions: Philosophical and Cultural Aspects*, ed. Edmund D. Pellegrino, Robert M. Veach, and John P. Langam (Washington, D.C.: Georgetown University Press, 1991), 69.

23. Baier, *Moral Prejudices,* 103.

24. Contract attorneys themselves make this point when they remind their clients that a contract cannot cover every unforeseen condition. Sometimes they cite for their clients examples of what will forever remain unknown. When clients realize that they cannot foresee premature endings, crises, shifts in power, and the like, they often turn back once again to the work of building trust with their partners. We can generalize from contract law to trust in general. When people reach the point of realizing how much of their formal agreements they cannot control, or how limited the help of a third party really is, they turn back again to face each other. They become aware of the need to tend to the health of their relationship.

25. Barbara J. Blodgett, *Constructing the Erotic: Sexual Ethics and Adolescent Girls* (Cleveland: Pilgrim, 2002), 168.

26. See Onora O'Neill, *A Question of Trust* (Cambridge: Cambridge University Press, 2002).

27. Jürgen Moltmann, "Control is Good, but Trust is Better," keynote address for "A Crisis of Trust? Trust in a Culture of Suspicion and Spin," Yale Divinity School, New Haven, Conn., September 17, 2004.

28. Axelrod, *The Evolution of Cooperation.*

29. Baier, *Moral Prejudices,* 149.

30. Margaret A. Farley, *Personal Commitments: Beginning, Keeping, Changing* (San Francisco: Harper & Row, 1986), 58–60.

2. CONFIDENTIALITY

1. D. Gene Kraus, "Confidentiality in the United Church of Christ: Some Theological Reflections" (Cleveland: United Church of Christ Parish Life and Leadership Ministry Team, February 2002), 1–2.

2. Don Clark, "Emerging Legal Issues in Contemporary Parish Ministry: An overview of recent judicial and legislative developments with implications for parish ministry, including a legal primer on confidentiality and best practices to ensure safe and effective church ministry" (address to the Connecticut Conference UCC 137th Annual Meeting, Suffield, Conn., October 15, 2004).

3. I follow Sissela Bok here, who advises: "The best policy is to be quite sparing in one's promises of secrecy about any information, but scrupulous, once having given such a promise, in respecting it." Sissela Bok, *Secrets: On the Ethics of Concealment and Revelation* (New York: Vintage, 1983), 95.

4. Kraus, "Confidentiality in the United Church of Christ," 7.

5. Joseph E. Bush Jr., *Gentle Shepherding: Pastoral Ethics and Leadership* (St. Louis: Chalice, 2006), 110.

6. Leland C. Swenson, "Confidentiality," in *Ready Reference Ethics,* vol. 1 (Pasadena: Salem, 1994), 181.

7. D. Elizabeth Audette, "Confidentiality in the Church: What the Pastor Knows and Tells," *The Christian Century* 115, no. 3 (January 28, 1998): 83.

8. D. Elizabeth Audette, "Does Only Your Minister Know? Religious, Legal Confidentiality Differ," *The Congregationalist* 158, no. 2 (April/May 1998): 19.

9. Bush, *Gentle Shepherding,* 110.

10. H. Newton Malony, "Confidentiality in the Pastoral Role," in *Clergy Malpractice*, ed. H. Newton Malony, Thomas L. Needham, and Samuel Southard (Philadelphia: Westminster, 1986), 117–18.

11. Audette, "Confidentiality in the Church," 83.

12. Ibid. A few years back I was having coffee with a ministerial colleague in a busy coffee house in the center of town a block away from his church. We were seated in the middle of the room. I asked him about his ethics of confidentiality, and he replied by using our coffee conversation as an example: anything I were to say that day he would keep confidential, because he was an ordained minister.

13. One legal commentator put it rather flatly: "If a teacher or minister were subpoenaed, placed on the stand, and asked for confidential information, most judges would require the person to answer. Except in cases involving priests in sacramental confession, ministers do not have the privilege of refusing to answer questions asked under oath." Mary Angela Shaughnessy, *Ministers and the Law: What You Need to Know* (New York: Paulist, 1998), 54.

14. Bush, *Gentle Shepherding*, 110.

15. Order for Ordination to Ministry, *United Church of Christ Book of Worship* (New York: United Church of Christ Office for Church Life and Leadership, 1986), 408. D. Gene Kraus points out, however, that certain ethical codes of the denomination reflect perhaps a less stringent standard. The Manual on Ministry, for example, calls upon authorized ministers to "honor all confidences shared with [them]." Cited in Kraus, "Confidentiality in the United Church of Christ," 4.

16. Dietrich Bonhoeffer, *Life Together*, trans. John W. Doberstein (San Francisco: Harper & Row, 1954), 110.

17. Ibid., 118.

18. Ibid., 113.

19. Ibid., 120.

20. William H. Willimon, "Heard About the Pastor Who . . . ? Gossip as an Ethical Activity," *The Christian Century* 107, no. 31 (October 31, 1990): 996.

21. Ibid.

22. Richard M. Gula, S.S., *Ethics in Pastoral Ministry* (New York: Paulist, 1996), 1.

23. Ibid., 130.

24. Ibid., 131.

25. Mary Beth Armstrong, "Confidentiality, General Issues of," in *Encyclopedia of Applied Ethics*, Vol. 1 (San Diego: Academic, 1998), 560.

26. Don McCoid, "AS I SEE IT: Confidentiality and Boundaries in the Church's Ministry: (Or) 'I Didn't Think That Applied to This Situation'," *Seminary Ridge Review* 3, no. 1 (Autumn 2000): 84.

27. Audette, "Confidentiality in the Church," 83.

28. See, for example, David A. Stoop, "Does 'Confidentiality' Have Limits? Relationships Between Pastors and Counselors," *American Journal of Pastoral Counseling* 3, no. 3/4 (2000): 37–44.

29. Bok, *Secrets*, 80.

30. Bonhoeffer, *Life Together*, 114.

31. Bok, *Secrets*, 81.

32. *Nally v. Grace Community Church of the Valley*, 47 Cal. 3d 278, 253 Cal. Rptr. 97, 763 P.2d 948 (Cal. Sup. Ct. 1988), 959. See William J. Beintema, *Clergy Malpractice: An Annotated Bibliography* (Buffalo: William S. Hein, 1990), 13–15.

33. Bok, *Secrets*, 84.

34. Bonhoeffer, *Life Together*, 120.

35. Another confidentiality risk is hearing something you do not particularly want to hear. Take, for example, the pastor who hears about misconduct on the part of a lay leader. Confidences like these can test our loyalties and challenge us to honor the unpleasant secret by facing it and taking necessary action.

36. Willimon, "Heard About the Pastor Who . . . ?" 996.

3. MISCONDUCT

1. Michael Power, *The Audit Society: Rituals of Verification* (Oxford: Oxford University Press, 1997).

2. Caroline Whitbeck, "Creating an Environment That Promotes Responsible Research Conduct," *A Publication from the Center for Professional Ethics at Case Western Reserve University* 4, no. 3 (Summer 2003): 1; http://www.case.edu/groups/cpe/issues/summer2003.pdf, accessed April 30, 2008.

3. Ibid., 2.

4. Onora O'Neill, *Autonomy and Trust in Bioethics* (Cambridge: Cambridge University Press, 2002), 129-30.

5. National Collaboration for Youth, *Screening Volunteers to Prevent Child Sexual Abuse: A Community Guide for Youth Organizations* (Washington, D.C.: The National Assembly of National Voluntary Health and Social Welfare Organizations, 1997), 17.

6. Steven W. Klipowicz, *Reducing the Risk of Child Sexual Abuse Training Manual* (Carol Stream, Ill.: Church Law & Tax Report, 1993), 8.

7. Lois Rifner, "We Won't Let it Happen Here! Preventing Child Sexual Abuse in the Church" in Beth Basham and Sara Lisberness, eds., *Striking Terror No More: The Church Responds to Domestic Violence* (Louisville: Bridge Resources, 1997), 9.

8. I was once giving a presentation on safe church practices and suggested that one form of "safety" was to have clear job descriptions for all those who exercise leadership in the church. A parishioner remarked what a good idea this would be on other grounds. She might actually know what her job description was!

9. *Screening Volunteers*, 19.

10. Joy Thornburg Melton, *Safe Sanctuaries: Reducing the Risk of Child Abuse in the Church* (Nashville: Discipleship Resources, 1998), 33. Of course, this only works if the windows remain uncovered. I once worked in an environment where staff members routinely put artwork all over the glass, or installed mini-blinds.

11. There are many resources now available advising churches on these practices. Among them, see Melton, *Safe Sanctuaries*, chap. 4; and Beth Swagman, *Preventing Child Abuse* (Grand Rapids: CRC Publications, 1995), chap. 1.

12. Klipowicz, *Reducing the Risk*, 7.

13. Jan Erickson-Pearson, *Safe Connections: What Parishioners can do to Understand and Prevent Clergy Sexual Abuse* (Chicago: Evangelical Lutheran Church in America Division for Ministry, 1996), 11.

14. Ibid., 50.

15. Self-care is simply too subjective and complex. I recently took a self-care inventory and scored exceptionally well. Since I know myself better than whoever designed the inventory, however, I know that my score did not genuinely reflect exceptional self-caring habits on my part. It felt like acing a test while knowing that the right questions were not asked.

16. Power, *The Audit Society,* 140.

17. Ibid., 20.

18. Ibid., 60.

19. Is this simply an example of conflict of interest? Technically, conflicts of interest involve dual loyalties. Auditors do not, however, stand to gain anything from members of the organization if the audit is favorable. Rather, their conflict is between presenting a positive or negative view to the principal.

20. Power, *The Audit Society,* 22.

21. M. Parker and D. Jary, "The McUniversity: Organizations, Management and Academic Subjectivity," *Organization* 2, no. 2 (1995): 319–38, cited in ibid., 103.

22. Power, *The Audit Society,* 13.

23. J. Van Maanen and B. Pentland, "Cops and Auditors: The Rhetoric of Records," in Sl. Sitkin and R. Bies, eds., *The Legalistic Organization* (Thousand Oaks, Calif.: Sage, 1994), 54. Quoted in ibid., 127.

24. Interestingly, Power notes that auditing firms that produce too many negative reports are fired or threatened with legal action! Does this not suggest that the desire for comfort is deeper than the desire for communication?

25. Power, *The Audit Society,* 135–36.

26. O'Neill, *Autonomy and Trust in Bioethics,* 122.

27. Ibid., 123.

28. Power, *The Audit Society,* 123.

29. O'Neill, *Autonomy and Trust in Bioethics,* 131.

30. Ibid., 141. Power even suggests that audits make the Cassandras of the world less worthy of our trust over time: "Assumptions of [m]istrust sustaining audit processes may be self-fulfilling as auditees adapt their behaviour strategically in response to the audit process, thereby becoming less trustworthy." Power, *The Audit Society,* 135.

31. See Diego Gambetta, "Can we Trust Trust?" in Gambetta, ed., *Trust: Making and Breaking Cooperative Relations* (Oxford: Basil Blackwell, 1988).

32. I had been one of the leaders of our church's youth group for several months when a parent asked me what had brought me to church that evening.

33. The youth group in my church drafted a covenant at their inaugural meeting, wrote it up in colorful ink, and then hung it on the wall. To this day they will refer occasionally to some point in the covenant, drawing each other's attention only half-jokingly to an infringement someone has committed.

34. Annette Baier, *Moral Prejudices: Essays on Ethics* (Cambridge, Mass.: Harvard University Press, 1994), 163.

35. Ibid., 165.

36. Ibid., 200.

37. Rodney J. Hunter, "Preaching Forgiveness in a Therapeutic Age," *Journal for Preachers* (Lent 2005): 29.

38. Marie M. Fortune, *Is Nothing Sacred? The Story of a Pastor, The Women He Sexually Abused, and the Congregation He Nearly Destroyed* (Cleveland: United Church Press, 1989), 157n25.

39. Baier, *Moral Prejudices,* 150.

40. Ibid., 193.

41. Rifner and Smith, "We Won't Let it Happen Here!," 3.

4. GOSSIP

1. Sissela Bok, *Secrets: On the Ethics of Concealment and Revelation* (New York: Vintage, 1983), 90.

2. Aaron Ben-Ze'ev, "The Vindication of Gossip," in *Good Gossip*, ed. Robert F. Goodman and Aaron Ben-Ze'ev (Lawrence: University Press of Kansas, 1994), 11.

3. Gabriele Taylor, "Gossip as Moral Talk," in Goodman and Ben-Ze'ev, eds., *Good Gossip*, 35.

4. Bok, *Secrets*, 93.

5. Patricia Meyer Spacks, *Gossip* (New York: Knopf, 1985), 6. Here, Spacks traces the mutual overlapping influences of the practice of gossip and the writing of novels.

6. Taylor, "Gossip as Moral Talk," 36.

7. Jörg R. Bergmann, *Discreet Indiscretions: The Social Organization of Gossip*, trans. John Bednarz Jr. (New York: Aldine de Gruyter, 1993), 48.

8. Ben-Ze'ev, "The Vindication of Gossip," 16.

9. Bergmann, *Discreet Indiscretions,* 153.

10. Richard Lischer, *Open Secrets: A Memoir of Faith and Discovery* (New York: Broadway, 2001), 93.

11. Ibid., 94.

12. Ibid., 99.

13. Ibid., 96.

14. Kathleen Norris, *Dakota: A Spiritual Geography* (New York: Houghton Mifflin, 1993), 72.

15. Ibid., 73–75.

16. Ibid., 73.

17. Ibid., 75.

18. Ibid.

19. Ibid., 76.

20. William Willimon, "'Heard About the Pastor Who . . .': The Morality of Gossip," *The Christian Century* 107, no. 31 (Oct 31, 1990): 996.

21. Ibid.

22. Ibid.

23. Marianne E. Jaeger, Anne A. Skleder, Bruce Rind, and Ralph L. Rosnow, "Gossip, Gossipers, Gossipees," in Goodman and Ben-Ze'ev, eds., *Good Gossip*, 154.

24. Robert F. Goodman, introduction to Goodman and Ben-Ze'ev, eds., *Good Gossip*, 1.

25. Bergmann, *Discreet Indiscretions*, 49.

26. Ibid., 58.

27. Ibid., 67.

28. Ibid., 68.

29. Ibid., 81–82.

30. Ibid., 86–91.

31. Ibid., 90.

32. Ibid., 98–100.

33. Ibid., 80.

34. Randall C. Young, "There is Nothing Idle About It: Deference and Dominance in Gossip as a Function of Role, Personality, and Social Context," doctoral dissertation, University of California, Berkeley, 2001, 44.

35. Ibid., 20.

36. Ibid., 44.

37. Ibid., 49–50.

38. Ibid., 46.

39. Ibid., 48.

40. Jaeger, et al., "Gossip, Gossipers, Gossipees," 162.

41. Ibid., 166.

42. Thomas Luckmann, foreword to Bergmann, *Discreet Indiscretions*, x.

43. Taylor, "Gossip as Moral Talk," 41.

44. Holly Doy Wah Hom, "Gossip as a Vehicle for Value Comparison: The Development of Social Norms and Social Bonding through Moral Judgment," doctoral dissertation, University of Virginia, 2004, 100.

45. Young, "There is Nothing Idle About It," 66.

46. Roy F. Baumeister, Liqing Zhan, and Kathleen D. Vohs, "Gossip as Cultural Learning," *Review of General Psychology* 8, no. 2 (June 2004): 113.

47. Ibid., 120.

48. Ibid., 119.

49. Norris, *Dakota*, 79.

50. Ibid., 81.

51. Ibid., 82.

52. D. Eder and J. L. Enke, "The Structure of Gossip: Opportunities and Constraints on Collective Expression among Adolescents," *American Sociological Review* 56 (1991): 494–508, in Marion K. Underwood, *Social Aggression Among Girls* (New York: Guilford, 2003), 144.

53. Ibid., 501.

54. The findings of this study were later used by a psychologist consulting with educators on the problem of bullying in schools. Drawing upon Eder and Enke's work, she demonstrated that female gossip can be so vicious as to be nearly

as destructive to children as the physical violence more typical of boys, and thus gossip should be considered a form of bullying. In terms of strategies for stopping such verbal violence, she suggested that girls be coached in how to interrupt gossip. See Peter K. Smith, Debra Pepler, and Ken Rigby, eds., *Bullying in Schools: How Successful Can Interventions Be?* (Cambridge: Cambridge University Press, 2004).

55. Sarah R. Wert and Peter Salovey, "A Social Comparison Account of Gossip," *Review of General Psychology* 8, no. 2 (June 2004): 124, italics in original.

56. Eric K. Foster, "Research on Gossip: Taxonomy, Methods, and Future Directions," *Review of General Psychology* 8, no. 2 (June 2004): 94, italics in original.

57. Wert and Salovey, "A Social Comparison Account of Gossip," 134, italics in original.

58. Lyn Mikel Brown, *Girlfighting: Betrayal and Rejection among Girls* (New York: New York University Press, 2003), 6.

59. Ibid., 157.

60. Ibid., 6.

61. For example, girls receive constant social and cultural messages to control their weight. They internalize the idea that they should be able to control at will their bodies' appearance. But weight is, in fact, a very difficult thing to control. Hence, girls who happen to weigh less seize upon weight as a way to gain favorable comparison with other girls and thus a pretense of having gained power in a world that approves of slender females. Not surprisingly, then, it is a very frequent topic of girls' gossip (as we saw in the example, above, where one girl was called a "cow"). Girls gossip about weight to compare themselves to their friends, given their need for desirability in a culture that demands proof of it.

62. Brown, *Girlfighting*, 6.

63. Underwood, *Social Aggression Among Girls,* 4, italics added.

64. Brown, *Girlfighting,* 200.

65. Spacks, *Gossip,* 33.

66. Ibid., 45.

67. Maryann Ayim, "Knowledge Through the Grapevine: Gossip as Inquiry," in Goodman and Ben-Ze'ev, eds., *Good Gossip,* 99.

68. Ben-Ze'ev, "The Vindication of Gossip," 24.

69. Spacks, *Gossip,* 11.

70. Ibid.

71. Thomas Hoyt Jr., "Testimony," in Dorothy C. Bass, ed., *Practicing Our Faith: A Way of Life for a Searching People* (San Francisco: Jossey-Bass, 1997), 92.

72. Ibid., 94.

73. In the interest of full disclosure I should note that this is the congregation to which I belong.

74. Lillian Daniel, *Tell It Like It Is: Reclaiming the Practice of Testimony* (Herndon, Va.: Alban Institute, 2006), 147.

75. Ibid., 151.
76. Ibid., 147.
77. Ibid., 19–20.
78. Ibid., 141.
79. Ibid., 147.

5. BULLSHIT

1. Lynna Williams, "Personal Testimony," in *Texas Bound: Nineteen Texas Stories*, ed. Kay Cattarulla (Dallas: Southern Methodist University Press, 1994), 197.

2. Ibid.

3. Ibid., 193–94.

4. Ibid., 203.

5. Testimony and autobiography are alike in many ways and afford a rich comparison. Autobiography as a genre has been extensively studied and written about, and the temptation to include that literature here is great. Space will permit, however, only a few references.

6. See John Paul Eakin, ed., *The Ethics of Life Writing* (Ithaca, N.Y.: Cornell University Press, 2004). Several contributors to this volume speak to the ethical problem of autobiography's potential for harming others and the associated problem of the autobiographer's motivation—especially Claudia Mills, "Friendship, Fiction, and Memoir: Trust and Betrayal in Writing from One's Own Life"; Richard Freadman, "Decent and Indecent: Writing My Father's Life"; Nancy K. Miller, "The Ethics of Betrayal: Diary of a Memoirist"; and Alice Wexler, "Mapping Lives: 'Truth,' Life Writing, and DNA." Miller explains how even the most conscientious autobiographer risks embarrassing and even betraying other people: If "every account of the self includes relations with others, how can an autobiographer tell a story without betraying the other, without violating the other's privacy . . . without doing harm, but nonetheless telling the story *from one's own perspective*, which by virtue of being a published text exerts a certain power?" (153, italics in original).

7. Philippe Lejeune, *Le pacte autobiographique* (Paris: Seuil, 1975), 13–46, as cited in John Paul Eakin, *Fictions in Autobiography: Studies in the Art of Self-Invention* (Princeton, N. J.: Princeton University Press, 1985), 10. Lejeune is one of the earliest modern critics of autobiography. Eakin cites the "pact" Lejeune identified in reference to questions of fact versus fiction in autobiography. Most readers, Eakin points out, agree to believe that what they are reading is factual, even while they tacitly accept a measure of fiction. Thus, the relationship of reader to autobiographer (and by extension, listener to testifier) nicely exemplifies our notion of a trust relationship. Eakin writes: "Why would we bother to read it in the first place if we did not believe in autobiography as a primary expression of biographical

truth? Realizing this, most autobiographers refrain from any behavior that would disturb the delicate entente between writer and reader that Philippe Lejeune has described as the autobiographical pact; indeed, they are apt to encourage our trust in the historicity of their accounts lest we leave them in the lurch with their lives on their hands" (10).

8. See Paul Lauritzen, "Arguing with Life Stories: The Case of Rigoberta Menchú," in Eakin, *The Ethics of Life Writing*, 19–39. Rigoberta Menchú won the Nobel Peace Prize in 1992 for her work on behalf of social justice for the Mayan people of Guatemala. She had written a provocative and politically powerful life story entitled *I, Rigoberta Menchú* (London: Verso, 1984) in the tradition of Latin American *testimonio*, a genre that shares characteristics with autobiography, diary, and nonfiction novel. Some parts of the *testimonio* were later questioned for their veracity, prompting an ethical debate between her supporters and detractors. There have been many other instances of readers questioning the truth of autobiographical accounts. Oprah Winfrey and her book-club fans were recently let down by a best-selling memoir (James Frey, *A Million Little Pieces* [New York: Anchor, 2005]).

9. Williams, "Personal Testimony," 196.

10. It is fitting, in this regard, that Williams chooses to tell the story in the first person and assume a child's voice.

11. Williams, "Personal Testimony," 195.

12. Ibid., 198.

13. Ibid., 204.

14. Richard M. Gula, S.S., *Ethics in Pastoral Ministry* (New York: Paulist, 1996), 70–71.

15. William F. May, "Images that Shape the Public Obligations of the Minister," in *Clergy Ethics in a Changing Society: Mapping the Terrain*, ed. James P. Wind, Russell Burck, Paul F. Camenisch, and Dennis P. McCann (Louisville: Westminster John Knox, 1991), 81.

16. In my position as a field educator, I hear divinity students' stories develop over the course of their years in school, from the inarticulate fumbling answers about why they are attending seminary to the polished statements written upon graduation for their ecclesial bodies. Sometimes I cannot help but find the inarticulate fumblings more honest.

17. Once they become a member of the clergy, ministers are often called upon to defend their status as special and distinct and possessing of powers not shared by others. Ecclesial traditions vary widely, of course, in terms of how they understand the nature of ordained status. Some denominations recognize that an "ontological change" occurs upon ordination, for example, while others see the difference between clergy and lay as a functional one. Those distinctions do not directly concern us here, for we are primarily interested in the professional power

that affects trust relationships, a sort of power that all clergy share (and, for that matter, all leaders share whether they are ordained clergy or not).

18. William H. Willimon, *Calling and Character: Virtues of the Ordained Life* (Nashville: Abingdon, 2000), 69.

19. Ibid.

20. Gaylord Noyce, *Pastoral Ethics: Professional Responsibilities of the Clergy* (Nashville: Abingdon, 1988), 52.

21. Ibid.

22. Ibid., 53.

23. Ibid.

24. Ibid., 54.

25. Ibid., 63.

26. Eugene H. Peterson, *The Contemplative Pastor: Returning to the Art of Spiritual Direction* (Grand Rapids, Mich.: Eerdmans, 1989), 88–89.

27. I am reminded of an episode of *The West Wing* in which the president of the United States has to call the parents of two brothers who have been killed in an attack on American civilians overseas. His strategists gather in the Oval Office to suggest different ways he might "spin" the news to make it sound like the young men did not die in vain. In the end, he picks up the phone, places the call, and says, "I'm the father of three daughters. I have no idea what to say to you."

28. Gula, *Ethics in Pastoral Ministry,* 71.

29. Praying out loud is, along with preaching, at the top of my students' list of scary things they have to learn to do in their internships.

30. Noyce, *Pastoral Ethics,* 194.

31. Walter E. Wiest and Elwyn A. Smith, *Ethics in Ministry: A Guide for the Professional* (Minneapolis: Fortress Press, 1990), 168.

32. Ibid., 21.

33. Ibid., 22–23.

34. Ibid., 22.

35. Paul J. Griffiths, *Lying: An Augustinian Theology of Duplicity* (Grand Rapids, Mich.: Brazos, 2004), 25.

36. Immanuel Kant, *The Metaphysics of Morals*, trans. Mary Gregor (Cambridge: Cambridge University Press, 1991), 225. In his doctrine of virtue, Kant placed not lying under the duties one has to oneself.

37. Christine M. Korsgaard, "The Right to Lie: Kant on Dealing with Evil," *Philosophy and Public Affairs* (Fall 1986): 337.

38. Charles Fried, "On Lying," in *Right and Wrong* (Cambridge, Mass.: Harvard University Press, 1978), 67.

39. Ibid.

40. Immanuel Kant, *Lectures on Ethics*, trans. Peter Heath, ed. Peter Heath and J.B. Schneewind (New York: Cambridge University Press, 1997), 229.

41. Griffiths, *Lying,* 25.

42. He is famous for going so far as to say that you should not lie to protect your friend from the murderer who comes looking for him, for if your friend should unbeknownst to you escape out the back way and run into the man you have dismissed and get killed, you may be held responsible for his death! Immanuel Kant, "On a Supposed Right to Lie from Altruistic Motives," ed. and trans. Lewis White Beck and reprinted in Sissela Bok, *Lying: Moral Choice in Public and Private Life* by (New York: Vintage, 1979), 287.

43. St. Augustine, "Lying," in *Treatises on Various Subjects*, trans. Mary Sarah Muldowney, et al., ed. Roy J. Deferrari, (New York: Fathers of the Church, 1952), 78.

44. Harry G. Frankfurt, "On Bullshit," in *The Importance of What We Care About: Philosophical Essays* (Cambridge: Cambridge University Press, 1988), 117.

45. Now available from popular booksellers in malls around the country, *On Bullshit* has garnered attention in the press, both print and television. Maybe now people will start taking bullshit seriously.

46. Harry G. Frankfurt, *On Bullshit* (Princeton, N. J.: Princeton University Press, 2005), 3. Future citations will refer to this publication.

47. Ibid., 16–18.

48. Ibid., 42–43.

49. This is the feature of bullshit with which my ethics students seem to identify most readily. In the academic realm in which they operate, they think of bullshitting in connection with paper writing. They resort to bullshit in a paper when they do not really know or care about their argument. They write bullshit in order to "pull something over on" their teacher. As a teacher, one can only hope one has a good "bullshit meter" with which to detect this strategy!

50. Frankfurt, *On Bullshit,* 47.

51. Ibid., 56.

52. G. A. Cohen, "Deeper Into Bullshit," in *Contours of Agency: Essays on Themes from Harry Frankfurt*, ed. Sara Buss and Lee Overton (Cambridge, Mass.: MIT Press, 2002), 321–39.

53. Ibid., 333.

54. Ibid.

55. Frankfurt, *On Bullshit,* 36–37.

56. Ibid., 35–36.

57. Much has been written about the ethics of clergy professional power so I will not go into it deeply here. See especially Karen Lebacqz, *Professional Ethics: Power and Paradox* (Nashville: Abingdon, 1985) and William Willimon's chapter in *Calling and Character* entitled "Crossbearing and the Clergy," where he gives credit to Lebacqz.

58. Willimon, *Calling and Character,* 109.

59. Ibid., 105.

CONCLUSION

1. I would like to thank David H. Smith for his suggestion that I construct the conclusion this way. See his own example in *Entrusted: The Moral Responsibilities of Trusteeship* (Bloomington: Indiana University Press, 1995), 109–14.

Index

MINIONS

PAELLA!

Art by: Renaud **COLLIN**   Written by: Stéphane **LAPUSS'**

Based on the characters from Universal Pictures and Illumination Entertainment's 2010 animated theatrical motion picture, "Despicable Me", the 2013 animated theatrical motion picture entitled "Despicable Me 2", and the 2015 animated theatrical motion picture release presently entitled "Minions".

AVAILABLE IN HARDCOVER AND SOFTCOVER:
MINIONS VOLUME 1: BANANA!
MINIONS VOLUME 2: EVIL PANIC
MINIONS: VIVA LE BOSS!

AVAILABLE IN SOFTCOVER:
MINIONS: PAELLA!

TITAN COMICS

Editor TOLLY MAGGS
Senior Creative Editor DAVID LEACH
Managing Editor MARTIN EDEN
Art Director OZ BROWNE
Senior Production Controller JACKIE FLOOK
Production Controller PETER JAMES
Sales & Circulation Manager STEVE TOTHILL
Marketing Assistant GEORGE WICKENDEN

Publicist IMOGEN HARRIS
Commercial Manager MICHELLE FAIRLAMB
Head Of Rights JENNY BOYCE
Publishing Director DARRYL TOTHILL
Editorial Director DUNCAN BAIZLEY
Operations Director LEIGH BAULCH
Executive Director VIVIAN CHEUNG
Publisher NICK LANDAU

MINIONS: PAELLA!

ISBN: 9781787730243
Published by Titan Comics, a division of Titan Publishing Group Ltd.144 Southwark St. London, SE1 0UP.

Based on characters from Universal Pictures and Illumination Entertainment's 2010 animated theatrical motion picture, "Despicable Me", the 2013 animated theatrical motion picture entitled "Despicable Me 2", and the 2015 theatrical motion picture entitled "Minions".

A CIP catalogue record for this title is available from the British library.
First Edition March 2020

Printed in China

10 9 8 7 6 5 4 3 2 1

www.despicable.me   #DespicableMe
Despicable Me, Minion Made and all related marks and characters are trademarks and copyrights of Universal Studios. Minions © 2020 Universal City Studios LLC. All Rights Reserved.

6

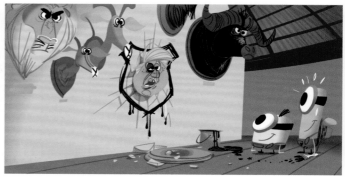

OÏNK

38

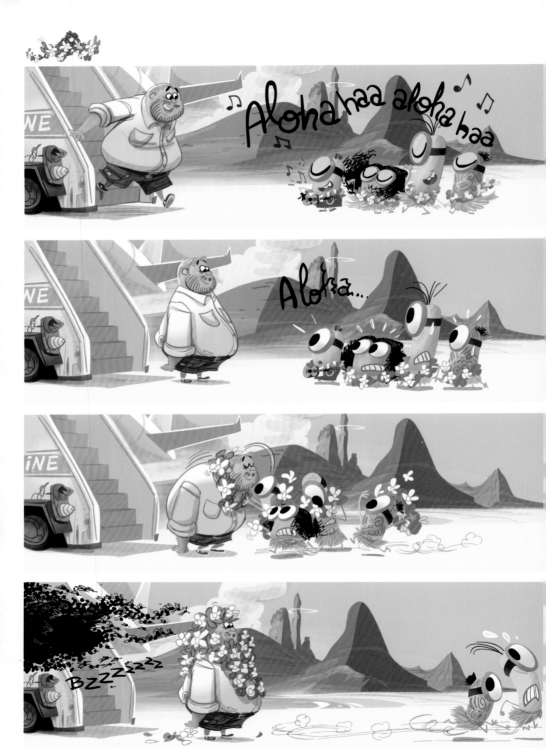

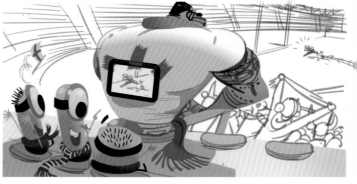